Guide to Food Storage

Follow this guide for food storage, and you can be sure that what's in your freezer, refrigerator, an⸮ ⸮⸮⸮⸮ is fresh-tasting and ready to use in recipes.

In the Freezer (at -10° to 0° F)

DAIRY

Cheese, hard ....6 months
Cheese, soft ....6 months
Egg substitute, unopened..1 year
Egg whites ....1 year
Egg yolks ....1 year
Ice cream, sherbet.. 1 month

FRUITS AND VEGETABLES

Commercially frozen fruits......................................1 year
Commercially frozen vegetables .... 8 to 12 months

MEATS, POULTRY, AND SEAFOOD

Beef, Lamb, Pork, and Veal

Chops, uncooked ....4 to 6 months
Ground and stew meat, uncooked ....3 to 4 months
Ham, fully cooked, half...................................1 to 2 months
Roasts, uncooked .... 4 to 12 months
Steaks, uncooked ....6 to 12 months

Poultry

All cuts, cooked ....4 months
Boneless or bone-in pieces, uncooked ....9 months

Seafood

Fish, fatty, uncooked ....2 to 3 months
Fish, lean, uncooked..6 months

In the Refrigerator (at 34° to 40° F)

DAIRY

Butter ....1 to 3 months
Buttermilk.. 1 to 2 weeks
Cheese, hard, wedge, opened....................................6 months
Cheese, semihard, block, opened............................ 3 to 4 weeks
Cream cheese, fat-free, light, and ⅓-less-fat..............2 weeks
Egg substitute, opened .... 3 days
Fresh eggs in shell ....3 to 5 weeks

MEATS, POULTRY, AND SEAFOOD

Beef, Lamb, Pork, and Veal

Ground and stew meat, uncooked ....1 to 2 days
Roasts, uncooked ....3 to 5 days
Steaks and chops, uncooked ....3 to 5 days

Chicken, Turkey, and Seafood

All cuts, uncooked...1 to 2 days

FRUITS AND VEGETABLES

Apples, beets, cabbage, carrots, celery,
   citrus fruits, eggplant, and parsnips................. 2 to 3 weeks
Apricots, asparagus, berries, cauliflower,
   cucumbers, mushrooms, okra, peaches,
   pears, peas, peppers, plums, salad greens,
   and summer squash......................................2 to 4 days
Corn, husked...1 day

In the Pantry (keep these at room temperature for 6 to 12 months)

BAKING AND COOKING STAPLES

Baking powder
Biscuit and baking mixes
Broth, canned
Cooking spray
Honey
Mayonnaise, fat-free, low-fat,
   and light (unopened)
Milk, canned evaporated fat-free
Milk, nonfat dry powder

Mustard, prepared (unopened)
Oils, olive and vegetable
Pasta, dried
Peanut butter
Rice, instant and regular
Salad dressings, bottled
   (unopened)
Seasoning sauces, bottled
Tuna, canned

FRUITS, LEGUMES, AND VEGETABLES

Fruits, canned
Legumes (beans, lentils, peas), dried or canned
Tomato products, canned
Vegetables, canned

WeightWatchers®

fresh
and easy
20 minute meals

Oxmoor
House®

ISBN-13: 978-0-8487-3280-6
ISBN-10: 0-8487-3280-4
Library of Congress Control Number: 2008935129
Printed in the United States of America
First printing 2009

Be sure to check with your health-care provider before making any changes in your diet.

Weight Watchers and **POINTS** are registered trademarks of Weight Watchers International, Inc., and are used under license by Oxmoor House, Inc.

Oxmoor House, Inc.

VP, Publishing Director: Jim Childs
Brand Manager: Victoria Alfonso
Managing Editor: L. Amanda Owens

Weight Watchers® Fresh and Easy 20 Minute Meals

Editor: Andrea C. Kirkland, M.S., R.D.
Project Editor: Diane Rose
Senior Designer: Emily Albright Parrish
Director, Test Kitchens: Elizabeth Tyler Austin
Assistant Director, Test Kitchens: Julie Christopher
Test Kitchens Professionals: Jane Chambliss, Kathleen Royal Phillips, Catherine Crowell Steele, Ashley T. Strickland, Deborah Wise
Photography Director: Jim Bathie
Senior Photo Stylist: Kay E. Clarke
Associate Photo Stylist: Katherine Eckert Coyne
Production Manager: Theresa Beste-Farley

Contributors

Designer and Compositor: Carol O. Loria
Copy Editor: Adrienne S. Davis
Proofreader: Carmine B. Loper
Indexer: Mary Ann Laurens
Recipe Development: David Bonom; Gretchen Feldtman Brown; Katherine Cobbs; Caroline Grant, M.S., R.D.; Alison Lewis; Debby Maugans; Jackie Mills, R.D.
Interns: Emily Chappell, Anne-Harris Jones, Shea Staskowski, Angela Valente
Food Stylist: Ana Price Kelly
Photographer: Beau Gustafson

Cover: Cumin-Rubbed Grilled Chicken with Nectarine Salsa (page 90)

Contents

Simple, Fresh Meals

Preparing delicious meals the whole family will love just got easier—thanks to this all-new *Fresh and Easy 20 Minute Meals* cookbook from Weight Watchers® Books. With more than 220 recipes, economical menus, step-by-step game plans, and **POINTS**® values, you'll find solutions that allow you to get nutritious meals on the table quickly and effortlessly without sacrificing your time or budget.

Essential Tips to Shop Smart and Cook Quick

Follow these straightforward strategies to master the art of cooking fresh, homemade menus fast and inexpensively.

Make meal plans.

• Set aside a little time each week to plan meals around your schedule on the nights you'll have time to cook.
• Take stock of the ingredients you have on hand and consider incorporating these items into your menus.
• Use our menus to speed up meal planning. Each menu in the book includes a main-dish recipe plus either a side-dish recipe or a "serve with" suggestion, such as a fruit, vegetable, bread, or grain to complete the meal. The **POINTS** values per serving are included with every menu and every recipe.

Manage your grocery budget.

• Establish a weekly grocery budget and adapt your menu choices to fit within that budget.
• Prepare a grocery list and commit to purchasing only the items on your list to prevent impulse purchases.
• Take advantage of store coupons, but make sure you use them to buy only the items you'll need.
• Purchase store-brand items instead of brand-name items when they're available and won't compromise the quality of the dish. Store-brand products usually cost less and are stocked on the top and bottom shelves in supermarkets.
• Plan to use prepared produce in more than one dish to make the most of its expense and to eliminate waste. Using prepared produce will save you time, but it can be a bit pricey. You'll save money by washing, chopping, slicing, and trimming produce yourself, but you'll need to add a few extra minutes to your prep time.

Multitask to save time.

• Gather all of your ingredients and kitchen equipment before you begin to prep or cook. While you're cooking, this step will allow you to complete more than one task at a time and reduce trips to the refrigerator and kitchen cupboards.
• Use the easy-to-follow game plans included with all menus to make the most of your kitchen time. Many of the menus include recipes with procedures that can be completed simultaneously. The game plans will guide you to chop and measure ingredients, toss a salad, or microwave something while you're waiting for water to boil or for the oven to preheat.

Purchase seasonal produce.
Shop the markets for seasonal fruits and vegetables while they're at their peak flavors and are selling at their lowest prices. Use the seasonal produce guide below to help you choose fresh produce for sensational meals year-round.

WINTER	SPRING	SUMMER	FALL
FRUITS			
Apples	Avocados	Apples	Cranberries
Cranberries	Berries	Avocados	Figs
Grapefruit	Grapefruit	Cherries	Grapes
Oranges	Mangoes	Grapes	Pears
Pears	Oranges	Mangoes	Pomegranates
Pomegranates	Pineapples	Melons	
	Strawberries	Peaches	
		Plums	
VEGETABLES			
Beets	Arugula	Bell peppers	Bell peppers
Brussels sprouts	Asparagus	Cabbage	Broccoli
Fennel	Avocados	Corn	Brussels sprouts
Mushrooms	Broccoli	Eggplant	Cabbage
Potatoes	Cauliflower	Green beans	Cauliflower
Sweet potatoes	Green peas	Okra	Eggplant
Turnips	Mushrooms	Summer squash	Fennel
Winter squash	Red potatoes	Tomatoes	Mushrooms
	Rhubarb		Shallots
			Sweet potatoes
			Winter squash

About the Recipes

Weight Watchers® *Fresh and Easy 20 Minute Meals* gives you the nutrition facts you need to stay on track. Every recipe in this book includes a **POINTS**® value. For more information on Weight Watchers, see page 5.

Each recipe has a list of nutrients—including calories, fat, percent of calories from fat, saturated fat, protein, carbohydrates, dietary fiber, cholesterol, iron, sodium, and calcium—as well as a serving size and the number of servings. This information makes it easy for you to use the recipes for any weight-loss program that you choose to follow. Measurements are abbreviated g (grams) and mg (milligrams). Nutritional values used in our calculations come from either The Food Processor, Version 8.9 (ESHA Research), or are provided by food manufacturers.

Numbers are based on these assumptions:

• Unless otherwise indicated, meat, poultry, and fish always refer to skinned, boned, and cooked servings.
• When we give a range for an ingredient (3 to 3½ cups flour, for instance), we calculate using the lesser amount.
• Some alcohol calories evaporate during heating; the analysis reflects this.
• Only the amount of marinade absorbed by the food is used in calculations.
• Garnishes and optional ingredients are not included in an analysis.

Safety Note: Cooking spray should never be used near direct heat. Always remove a pan from heat before spraying it with cooking spray.

A Note on Diabetic Exchanges: You may notice that the nutrient analysis for each recipe does not include Diabetic Exchanges. Most dietitians and diabetes educators are now teaching people with diabetes to count total carbohydrates at each meal and snack, rather than counting exchanges. Counting carbohydrates gives people with diabetes more flexibility in their food choices and seems to be an effective way to manage blood glucose.

Almost all of our recipes can be incorporated into a diabetic diet by using the carbohydrate amount in the nutrient analysis and incorporating that into the carbohydrate amount recommended by your physician.

POINTS values

The Momentum™ Program is based on the Weight Watchers **POINTS** Weight-Loss System and encourages you to focus on foods that will help you lose weight, feel fuller longer, and stay satisfied.
• Every food has a **POINTS** value that is based on calories, fat grams, and fiber grams in a specific portion of food.
• Members keep track of **POINTS** values and stick to their individual daily **POINTS** Target, which is the number of **POINTS** values a person needs to eat each day in order to lose weight.
• You can enjoy a full range of food options at home, on the go, or when dining out.

Breakfast

Menu
POINTS value
per serving: 6

**Strawberry and Banana
Breakfast Smoothie**

**Mini Bagels with
Honey-Nut Cream Cheese**

Game Plan

1. Rinse, drain, and slice strawberries.

2. While nuts and bagels toast:
   • Measure cream cheese, honey, and cinnamon.

3. Spread cream cheese mixture over bagels.

4. Prepare smoothie.

Strawberry and Banana Breakfast Smoothie

prep: 7 minutes   **POINTS** value: 3

Choose this energizing beverage—with nutrient-packed fruit, yogurt, and wheat germ—for a portable meal on the go or to sip while getting ready for work. For quicker preparation in the morning, stir together the ingredients for the cream cheese mixture the night before and refrigerate.

> 2   cups sliced strawberries
> 2   (6-ounce) cartons low-fat vanilla yogurt
> 1½   cups ice
> ½   cup fat-free milk
> 2   tablespoons toasted wheat germ
> 1   tablespoon maple syrup or honey
> 1   banana

1. Place all ingredients in a blender; process until smooth. Serve immediately.
Yield: 4 servings (serving size: about 1¼ cups).

Per serving: CALORIES 162 (9% from fat); FAT 1.6g (saturated fat 0.8g); PROTEIN 5.9g; CARBOHYDRATES 33g; FIBER 2.7g; CHOLESTEROL 6mg; IRON 0.8mg; SODIUM 68mg; CALCIUM 183mg

Mini Bagels with Honey-Nut Cream Cheese

prep: 4 minutes • **cook:** 3 minutes   **POINTS** value: 3

Slice and toast 4 (1.5-ounce) whole wheat mini bagels. Combine ¼ cup (2 ounces) tub-style light cream cheese, 1 tablespoon honey, and ⅛ teaspoon ground cinnamon in a bowl; stir in 4 teaspoons chopped and toasted pecans or walnuts. Spread cream cheese mixture evenly over cut sides of mini bagels. **Yield:** 4 servings (serving size: 2 mini bagel halves and about 1½ tablespoons cream cheese mixture).

Per serving: CALORIES 181 (27% from fat); FAT 5.4g (saturated fat 2.3g); PROTEIN 6.4g; CARBOHYDRATES 29.3g; FIBER 4.3g; CHOLESTEROL 10mg; IRON 1.5mg; SODIUM 292mg; CALCIUM 25mg

pictured on page 34

Berry and Granola Greek Yogurt Parfaits

prep: 7 minutes   *POINTS* value: 7

Buy fresh berries during the summer when they're in season and are less expensive. Then freeze them to enjoy months later. It's best to freeze the berries, unwashed, in a single layer on a baking sheet and then transfer them to a heavy-duty zip-top bag. In this recipe, we recommend using Greek fat-free yogurt, which is thicker, richer, and creamier than regular fat-free yogurt. Look for it in the dairy section of your supermarket.

  1   cup Greek fat-free yogurt, divided
  ½   cup whole grain granola (such as Bear Naked Peak Protein), divided
  ½   cup blackberries, divided
  ½   cup raspberries, divided
  ¼   cup honey, divided

1. Spoon ¼ cup yogurt into each of 2 small parfait glasses. Top each with 2 table-spoons granola, 2 tablespoons blackberries, and 2 tablespoons raspberries. Drizzle 1 tablespoon honey over each serving. Repeat layers once. Yield: 2 servings.

Per serving: CALORIES 361 (18% from fat); FAT 7.4g (saturated fat 0.5g); PROTEIN 15.9g; CARBOHYDRATES 62.6g; FIBER 5.9g; CHOLESTEROL 0mg; IRON 2.4mg; SODIUM 64mg; CALCIUM 116mg

Menu
POINTS value
per serving: 7

Berry and Granola Greek Yogurt Parfaits

Game Plan

1. Rinse and drain berries.

2. Assemble parfaits.

Menu
POINTS value
per serving: 7

Cherry-Almond Swiss Muesli

1 cup cubed pineapple
POINTS value: 1

Game Plan

1. Prepare oat mixture.

2. While oat mixture stands:
- Toast almonds.
- Spoon pineapple onto serving plates.

Cherry-Almond Swiss Muesli

prep: 8 minutes • **cook:** 2 minutes • **other:** 10 minutes   *POINTS* value: 6

Swiss muesli is typically served shortly after combining the oats with the wet ingredients, but you can also chill it at least 3 hours or overnight for a creamier texture. The mixture will become thicker as it stands. Before serving, stir in a small amount of soy milk to slightly thin the muesli.

2	cups old-fashioned rolled oats
3	(6-ounce) cartons peach fat-free yogurt (such as Dannon Light & Fit)
3	tablespoons chopped dried sweet cherries
2	tablespoons "measures-like-sugar" reduced-calorie brown sugar blend (such as Splenda)
¼	teaspoon salt
1	cup light vanilla soy milk (such as Silk)
2	tablespoons chopped almonds, toasted

1. Combine oats and next 5 ingredients in a medium bowl, stirring well. Let stand 10 minutes, stirring occasionally. Stir in almonds; serve immediately. **Yield:** 4 servings (serving size: 1 cup).

Per serving: CALORIES 326 (13% from fat); FAT 4.7g (saturated fat 0.3g); PROTEIN 13.4g; CARBOHYDRATES 55.5g; FIBER 5.2g; CHOLESTEROL 3mg; IRON 2.3mg; SODIUM 241mg; CALCIUM 252mg

Oatmeal with Apples and Raisins

prep: 7 minutes • **cook:** 10 minutes   *POINTS* value: 4

This warm homemade breakfast staple is chock-full of fruit and delicately spiced with ground cinnamon and vanilla. When compared to prepackaged flavored oatmeal, old-fashioned rolled oats purchased in a large canister are more budget-friendly. Store oats in an airtight container and they'll last for up to 6 months.

    3½   cups 1% low-fat milk
     2   cups old-fashioned rolled oats
    1½   cups chopped peeled Granny Smith apple (about 5.6 ounces)
    ¼   cup packed light brown sugar
    ¼   cup unpacked golden raisins
    ¼   teaspoon ground cinnamon
    ¼   teaspoon salt
    ½   teaspoon vanilla extract

1. Combine first 7 ingredients in a medium saucepan. Bring to a boil over medium-high heat, stirring frequently. Reduce heat to medium; simmer 5 minutes or until thick and creamy, stirring frequently.

2. Remove from heat, and stir in vanilla. Serve immediately. **Yield:** 6 servings (serving size: about 1 cup).

Per serving: CALORIES 230 (14% from fat); FAT 3.5g (saturated fat 1.2g); PROTEIN 8.7g; CARBOHYDRATES 43.8g; FIBER 3.6g; CHOLESTEROL 6mg; IRON 2mg; SODIUM 174mg; CALCIUM 202mg

Menu
POINTS value
per serving: 5

Oatmeal with Apples and Raisins

**1 (1-ounce) slice warm
Canadian bacon**
POINTS value: 1

Game Plan

1. Peel and chop apple.

2. Cook oatmeal.

3. While oatmeal cooks:
• Heat Canadian bacon according to package directions.

Cinnamon French Toast

prep: 3 minutes • **cook:** 4 minutes, 30 seconds per batch   *POINTS* value: 4

Caramelizing the cinnamon sugar onto the French toast slices adds sweetness and a nice crunchy texture. You may use 1 (5-ounce) can fat-free evaporated milk instead of the soy milk for a *POINTS* value of 5 per serving.

⅔ cup light vanilla soy milk (such as Silk)
½ cup egg substitute
1 teaspoon vanilla extract
Butter-flavored cooking spray
8 (1-ounce) slices 100% whole wheat bread (such as Nature's Own 100% Whole Wheat)
2 tablespoons cinnamon sugar
1 cup blueberries
½ cup sugar-free maple-flavored syrup (such as Mrs. Butterworth's)

1. Combine soy milk, egg substitute, and vanilla extract in a shallow dish, stirring with a whisk.

2. Heat a large nonstick griddle or nonstick skillet over medium heat. Coat pan with cooking spray. Dip bread slices in egg mixture, coating sides well. Place bread slices on griddle, and cook bottom sides 2 minutes or until golden brown. Turn bread slices; coat top sides with cooking spray, and sprinkle evenly with cinnamon sugar. Cook 2 minutes or until golden brown. Turn bread slices, and cook 30 seconds or until cinnamon sugar caramelizes. Serve immediately with blueberries and syrup. **Yield:** 4 servings (serving size: 2 bread slices, ¼ cup blueberries, and 2 tablespoons syrup).

Per serving: CALORIES 224 (20% from fat); FAT 4.9g (saturated fat 0.3g); PROTEIN 13.2g; CARBOHYDRATES 36.8g; FIBER 8.1g; CHOLESTEROL 0mg; IRON 3.1mg; SODIUM 400mg; CALCIUM 174mg

pictured on page 33

Banana–Whole Wheat Pancakes with Strawberry Syrup

prep: 5 minutes • **cook:** 4 minutes per batch   *POINTS* value: 4

Mashed banana on the inside of these fluffy pancakes makes them tender without the addition of a lot of fat. The banana slices on top double the flavor and pair well with the strawberries in the syrup.

    6   tablespoons all-purpose flour
    ¼   cup whole wheat flour
    1½ teaspoons baking powder
    ¼   teaspoon salt
    1   medium banana, halved crosswise
    1   large egg
    ½   cup vanilla soy milk (such as Silk)
    1   tablespoon nonhydrogenated buttery spread (such as Smart Balance), melted
        Cooking spray
    1   cup frozen unsweetened whole strawberries or fresh strawberries
    ¼   cup sugar-free maple-flavored syrup (such as Mrs. Butterworth's)

1. Lightly spoon flours into dry measuring cups; level with a knife. Combine flours, baking powder, and salt in a medium bowl, stirring with a whisk.
2. Mash half of banana with a fork to measure ¼ cup. Combine mashed banana and egg, stirring with a whisk until blended. Add soy milk and buttery spread, stirring with a whisk; add to flour mixture, stirring until smooth.
3. Heat a large nonstick griddle or nonstick skillet over medium heat. Coat pan with cooking spray. Pour ¼ cup batter per pancake onto pan. Cook 2 to 3 minutes or until tops are covered with bubbles and edges look cooked. Carefully turn pancakes over, and cook 2 to 3 minutes or until bottoms are lightly browned.
4. While pancakes cook, combine strawberries and syrup in a 1-cup glass measure; cover and microwave at HIGH 1 minute or until warm. Cut remaining banana half into 18 thin slices. Serve pancakes with banana slices and strawberry syrup.
Yield: 3 servings (serving size: 2 pancakes, 6 banana slices, and ¼ cup syrup).

Per serving: CALORIES 226 (22% from fat); FAT 5.6g (saturated fat 1.5g); PROTEIN 6.8g; CARBOHYDRATES 41g; FIBER 3.8g; CHOLESTEROL 71mg; IRON 2.3mg; SODIUM 558mg; CALCIUM 209mg

Menu
POINTS value
per serving: 5

Banana–Whole Wheat Pancakes with Strawberry Syrup

1 cup fat-free milk
POINTS value: 1

Game Plan

1. Measure dry ingredients for pancakes.

2. Prepare mashed banana for pancake mixture and banana slices to top pancakes.

3. While pancakes cook:
  • Prepare syrup.

Menu

POINTS value
per serving: 8

**Banana Cream–Topped Waffles
with Blueberry Syrup**

Spiced Bacon

Game Plan

1. Rinse and drain blueberries.

2. Prepare syrup.

3. While bacon cooks:
  • Prepare yogurt mixture.

4. Toast waffles.

Banana Cream–Topped Waffles with Blueberry Syrup

prep: 8 minutes • **cook:** 3 minutes   **POINTS** value: 6

Adding fresh blueberries to prepared syrup enhances the flavor and boosts your intake of disease-fighting antioxidants that may help prevent cancer and heart disease.

¼ cup (2 ounces) block-style ⅓-less-fat cream cheese, softened
3 tablespoons powdered sugar
1 (6-ounce) carton banana cream pie low-fat yogurt
2 cups sliced banana (about 2 medium)
½ cup blueberries
¼ cup blueberry syrup (such as Knotts Berry Farm Syrup)
8 low-fat whole grain waffles (such as Kashi GOLEAN)

1. Combine cream cheese and powdered sugar in a medium bowl; beat with mixer at medium speed 2 minutes or until smooth. Add yogurt; beat 1 minute or until well blended. Fold in banana.
2. Combine blueberries and syrup in a microwave-safe bowl. Microwave at HIGH 1 to 2 minutes or until mixture boils, stirring after 1 minute.
3. Toast waffles in oven according to package directions. Top waffles with yogurt mixture, and drizzle with blueberry syrup. **Yield:** 4 servings (serving size: 2 waffles, ½ cup yogurt mixture, and 2 tablespoons blueberry syrup).

Per serving: CALORIES 334 (13% from fat); FAT 4.8g (saturated fat 1g); PROTEIN 11.1g; CARBOHYDRATES 67.3g; FIBER 6.9g; CHOLESTEROL 8mg; IRON 1.5mg; SODIUM 403mg; CALCIUM 122mg

Spiced Bacon

prep: 4 minutes • **cook:** 8 minutes   **POINTS** value: 2

Combine 2 tablespoons dark brown sugar, ¼ teaspoon ground cinnamon, ⅛ teaspoon ground cloves, and ⅛ teaspoon ground red pepper. Rub sugar mixture over both sides of 8 slices center-cut bacon. Heat a large nonstick skillet over medium heat. Coat pan with cooking spray. Cook bacon until crisp, turning occasionally. **Yield:** 4 servings (serving size: 2 slices).

Per serving: CALORIES 67 (36% from fat); FAT 2.7g (saturated fat 1g); PROTEIN 4g; CARBOHYDRATES 6.9g; FIBER 0.1g; CHOLESTEROL 10mg; IRON 0.2mg; SODIUM 176mg; CALCIUM 8mg

Baked Eggs with Tomatoes and Artichokes

prep: 4 minutes · **cook:** 13 minutes   *POINTS* value: 3

Tomatoes and chives infuse garden-fresh flavor into this delightful rise-and-shine dish.

  2   teaspoons butter
  1   (1.6-ounce) slice multigrain bread (such as Arnold Healthy Multigrain), cut into 4 pieces
  4   canned artichoke bottoms
  1   plum tomato, cut into 4 thick slices
  ½   teaspoon chopped fresh chives, divided
  4   large eggs
  ¼   teaspoon salt
  ¼   teaspoon freshly ground black pepper

1. Preheat oven to 375°.
2. Rub ½ teaspoon butter on bottom and up sides of each of 4 (4-ounce) ramekins or custard cups.
3. Press 1 bread piece into each of 4 ramekins. Top bread pieces evenly with artichoke bottoms, tomato slices, and ¼ teaspoon chives. Break 1 egg on top of tomato mixture in each ramekin. Sprinkle each evenly with remaining ¼ teaspoon chives, salt, and pepper. Bake at 375° for 13 minutes or until desired degree of doneness. Serve immediately. **Yield:** 4 servings (serving size: 1 ramekin).

Per serving: CALORIES 113 (57% from fat); FAT 7.1g (saturated fat 2.8g); PROTEIN 7.5g; CARBOHYDRATES 5.1g; FIBER 1g; CHOLESTEROL 217mg; IRON 1.2mg; SODIUM 325mg; CALCIUM 35mg

Cantaloupe with Honey and Lime

prep: 5 minutes   *POINTS* value: 1

Cut ½ cantaloupe into 4 wedges. Cut slits into each wedge, cutting into but not through rind. Drizzle each wedge with 1 teaspoon honey and 1 teaspoon lime juice. Serve immediately. **Yield:** 4 servings (serving size: 1 wedge).

Per serving: CALORIES 46 (2% from fat); FAT 0.1g (saturated fat 0g); PROTEIN 0.6g; CARBOHYDRATES 11.9g; FIBER 0g; CHOLESTEROL 0mg; IRON 0.2mg; SODIUM 11mg; CALCIUM 7mg

---

Menu
POINTS value
per serving: 6

Baked Eggs with Tomatoes and Artichokes

Cantaloupe with Honey and Lime

1 (6-ounce) carton lemon fat-free yogurt
POINTS value: 2

Game Plan

1. While oven preheats:
 • Prepare eggs.

2. While eggs bake:
 • Prepare cantaloupe.

Menu
POINTS value
per serving: 5

**Tomato, Spinach, and
Goat Cheese Frittata**

**1 cup red seedless grapes
POINTS** value: 1

Game Plan

1. Rinse and drain grapes.

2. While broiler preheats:
- Chop shallots, tomatoes, and basil.
- Cook vegetable mixture.
- Cook egg mixture.

3. Broil frittata.

Tomato, Spinach, and Goat Cheese Frittata

prep: 6 minutes • **cook:** 13 minutes   **POINTS** value: 4

You'll love the distinctive, mild flavor that creamy goat cheese lends to this frittata. For a bolder taste, try making this recipe with feta cheese.

Butter-flavored cooking spray
½   cup sliced fresh mushrooms
2   tablespoons finely chopped shallots
4   large eggs
2   large egg whites
¼   teaspoon salt
¼   teaspoon black pepper
½   (6-ounce) package fresh baby spinach
1¼ cups cherry tomatoes, quartered
¼   cup crumbled goat cheese
2   tablespoons chopped fresh basil

1. Preheat broiler.
2. Heat a large oven-proof skillet over medium heat. Coat pan with cooking spray. Add mushrooms and shallots to pan. Cook 3 minutes or until tender, stirring occasionally.
3. While mushroom mixture cooks, combine eggs, egg whites, salt, and pepper in a large bowl, stirring with a whisk.
4. Add spinach to mushroom mixture; cook 1 minute or until wilted, stirring constantly. Reduce heat to low. Pour egg mixture over vegetable mixture. As mixture starts to cook, gently lift edges of frittata with a spatula, and tilt pan so uncooked portion flows underneath. Cook 3 minutes; remove from heat. Sprinkle tomato and cheese over frittata.
5. Broil frittata 5 minutes or until set and lightly browned. Sprinkle with basil. Cut frittata into 4 wedges. **Yield:** 4 servings (serving size: 1 wedge).

Per serving: CALORIES 155 (56% from fat); FAT 9.7g (saturated fat 4.5g); PROTEIN 12.6g; CARBOHYDRATES 5.2g; FIBER 1.1g; CHOLESTEROL 223mg; IRON 2.1mg; SODIUM 339mg; CALCIUM 98mg

Leek and Asparagus Frittata

prep: 7 minutes • **cook:** 8 minutes   *POINTS* value: 3

Herbes de Provence is a blend of rosemary, marjoram, basil, bay leaves, thyme, and lavender and is commonly used in cuisine from the south of France. Look for it on the spice aisle at your supermarket.

- 1   tablespoon olive oil
- 1   cup sliced leek
- 1½   cups (1-inch) sliced asparagus
- 3   large egg whites
- 2   large eggs
- 1   teaspoon Herbes de Provence
- ¼   teaspoon salt
- ⅛   teaspoon freshly ground black pepper
- ½   cup grated Parmesan cheese, divided

1. Preheat broiler.

2. Heat oil in a large oven-proof skillet over medium-high heat. Add leek and asparagus to pan; sauté 3 minutes or until browned.

3. While leek mixture cooks, combine egg whites and the next 4 ingredients in a medium bowl, stirring with a whisk. Stir in ¼ cup cheese.

4. Reduce heat to low. Pour egg mixture over vegetable mixture. As mixture starts to cook, gently lift edges of frittata with a spatula, and tilt pan so uncooked portion flows underneath. Cook 2 to 3 minutes, and remove from heat. Sprinkle remaining ¼ cup cheese over frittata.

5. Broil frittata 2 minutes or until set and lightly browned. Cut into 4 wedges.

Yield: 4 servings (serving size: 1 wedge).

Per serving: CALORIES 142 (57% from fat); FAT 9g (saturated fat 3g); PROTEIN 10.8g; CARBOHYDRATES 4.8g; FIBER 1.1g; CHOLESTEROL 115mg; IRON 1.7mg; SODIUM 379mg; CALCIUM 148mg

Broiled Grapefruit

prep: 2 minutes • **cook:** 7 minutes   *POINTS* value: 1

Preheat broiler. Cut 2 medium-sized pink grapefruit in half crosswise. Place grapefruit halves on a baking sheet. Sprinkle each half with 1½ teaspoons turbinado sugar. Broil 7 minutes or until lightly browned and sugar melts. Serve each grapefruit half with 1 tablespoon Greek fat-free yogurt. **Yield:** 4 servings (serving size: 1 grapefruit half).

Per serving: CALORIES 90 (0% from fat); FAT 0g (saturated fat 0g); PROTEIN 2.2g; CARBOHYDRATES 21.6g; FIBER 2g; CHOLESTEROL 0mg; IRON 0mg; SODIUM 5mg; CALCIUM 50mg

---

Menu
POINTS value
per serving: 4

Leek and Asparagus Frittata

Broiled Grapefruit

Game Plan

1. While broiler preheats:
- Halve grapefruit, and sprinkle with sugar.
- Slice vegetables.

2. While grapefruit cooks:
- Cook vegetable mixture.
- Cook egg mixture.

3. Broil frittata.

pictured on page 35

Smoked Salmon–Spinach Omelet

prep: 2 minutes • **cook:** 10 minutes   *POINTS* value: 6

Salty smoked salmon and robust Cheddar cheese transform humble eggs into an easy, elegant brunch dish that's perfect to serve guests.

Cooking spray
2 cups sliced fresh mushrooms
3 cups fresh baby spinach
1 (4-ounce) package smoked salmon, chopped
⅛ teaspoon black pepper
4 large eggs
4 large egg whites
1 tablespoon fat-free milk
1 cup (4 ounces) shredded reduced-fat 2% Cheddar cheese
¼ cup reduced-fat sour cream
1 tablespoon chopped fresh parsley

1. Heat a nonstick skillet over medium-high heat. Coat pan with cooking spray. Add mushrooms to pan; cook 4 minutes, stirring often. Add spinach, and cook 1 minute or until wilted, stirring constantly. Stir in salmon and pepper; cook 1 minute or just until salmon is thoroughly heated. Remove from pan; cover and keep warm.
2. Combine eggs, egg whites, and milk in a large bowl, stirring with a whisk.
3. Recoat pan with cooking spray, and place over medium-high heat. Add egg mixture to pan; cook until edges begin to set (about 2 minutes). Gently lift edge of omelet with a spatula, and tilt pan so uncooked portion flows underneath. Cook 1 minute or until center is set.
4. Spoon salmon filling down center of omelet; top with cheese. Loosen omelet with a spatula; fold in half. Carefully slide omelet onto serving platter, and cut into 4 wedges. Serve with sour cream and parsley. **Yield:** 4 servings (serving size: ¼ omelet, 1 tablespoon sour cream, and about ¾ teaspoon parsley).

Per serving: CALORIES 259 (50% from fat); FAT 14.4g (saturated fat 7g); PROTEIN 25.2g; CARBOHYDRATES 6.2g; FIBER 0.5g; CHOLESTEROL 246mg; IRON 2.6mg; SODIUM 639mg; CALCIUM 310mg

Pear and Grape Salad

prep: 5 minutes • **cook:** 2 minutes   *POINTS* value: 2

Combine 2½ tablespoons balsamic vinegar, 1 teaspoon olive oil, ½ teaspoon sugar, and a dash of black pepper in a small bowl, stirring with a whisk. Core and slice 1 red and 1 green pear. Halve 1 cup red grapes. Place pears and grapes in a bowl, and drizzle with dressing; toss gently to coat. Spoon salad onto a serving plate; sprinkle evenly with 2 tablespoons crumbled blue cheese and 1 tablespoon toasted pecans. **Yield:** 4 servings (serving size: about ¾ cup salad).

Per serving: CALORIES 88 (40% from fat); FAT 3.9g (saturated fat 1.1g); PROTEIN 1.6g; CARBOHYDRATES 12.7g; FIBER 2.6g; CHOLESTEROL 3mg; IRON 0.2mg; SODIUM 62mg; CALCIUM 31mg

Menu
POINTS value
per serving: 8

Smoked Salmon–Spinach Omelet

Pear and Grape Salad

Game Plan

1. While mushrooms cook:
• Toast pecans.
• Chop parsley and salmon.

2. While eggs cook:
• Make dressing.
• Slice pears, and halve grapes.

Veggie-Egg Scramble

prep: 2 minutes • **cook:** 9 minutes   *POINTS* value: 3

Prechopped veggies and a cilantro herb blend make this flavorful morning mixture speedy to prepare. The cilantro herb blend is packaged in a tube and found alongside the fresh herbs in the produce section of your supermarket. Plan to use any extra prechopped tricolor bell pepper mix to prepare Fattoush Salad on page 111.

page 111

2	teaspoons olive oil
½	cup prechopped onion
¼	cup prechopped tricolor bell pepper mix
½	cup broccoli florets, coarsely chopped
1	cup egg substitute
2	teaspoons cilantro herb blend (such as Gourmet Garden)
¼	teaspoon salt
⅛	teaspoon freshly ground black pepper
½	cup (2 ounces) crumbled goat cheese

1. Heat oil in a large nonstick skillet over medium heat. Add onion, bell pepper mix, and broccoli to pan; cook 5 minutes or until tender, stirring occasionally.
2. While vegetables cook, combine egg substitute and next 3 ingredients in a small bowl, stirring with a whisk. Add egg mixture to vegetable mixture; cook 2 minutes or until eggs are soft-scrambled, stirring frequently.
3. Divide egg mixture among 4 serving plates; sprinkle evenly with cheese. Serve immediately. **Yield:** 4 servings (serving size: ¼ of egg mixture and ½ ounce cheese).

Per serving: CALORIES 140 (56% from fat); FAT 8.7g (saturated fat 3.7g); PROTEIN 11.1g; CARBOHYDRATES 4g; FIBER 0.7g; CHOLESTEROL 12mg; IRON 1.7mg; SODIUM 366mg; CALCIUM 85mg

Apricot White Tea

prep: 3 minutes • **cook:** 3 minutes • **other:** 5 minutes   *POINTS* value: 2

Bring 2 cups of water to a boil; remove from heat. Add 2 white tea bags (such as Salada); cover and steep 5 minutes. Remove and discard tea bags. Add 1½ tablespoons sugar, stirring with a whisk until dissolved. Stir in 4 (5.5-ounce) cans apricot nectar and 1½ teaspoons lemon juice. Serve warm or over ice with a lemon slice, if desired. **Yield:** 4 servings (serving size: about 1¼ cups).

Per serving: CALORIES 112 (1% from fat); FAT 0.1g (saturated fat 0g); PROTEIN 0.6g; CARBOHYDRATES 29.4g; FIBER 0.9g; CHOLESTEROL 0mg; IRON 0.6mg; SODIUM 5mg; CALCIUM 11mg

---

Menu
POINTS value
per serving: 7

Veggie-Egg Scramble

Apricot White Tea

1 whole wheat English muffin, toasted
POINTS value: 2

Game Plan

1. While water comes to a boil for tea:
   - Heat oil in skillet.
   - Chop broccoli, and measure prechopped vegetables.

2. While tea steeps and vegetables cook:
   - Prepare egg mixture.

3. While egg mixture cooks:
   - Combine tea, sugar, nectar, and lemon juice.

Menu
POINTS value
per serving: 5

Bacon and Egg Sandwiches with Basil Mayonnaise

1 cup cubed watermelon
POINTS value: 1

Game Plan

1. While broiler preheats:
  • Chop basil.
  • Slice tomato.
  • Cook bacon.

2. While bread toasts:
  • Cook eggs.

3. Assemble sandwiches, and spoon watermelon into serving bowls.

Bacon and Egg Sandwiches with Basil Mayonnaise

prep: 6 minutes • **cook:** 7 minutes

POINTS value: 4

This recipe updates simple bacon and egg sandwiches by adding fresh basil and a juicy sliced tomato. Accompany the sandwiches with ripe melon cubes to complete the meal.

¼ cup light mayonnaise
2 tablespoons chopped fresh basil
½ teaspoon fresh lemon juice
4 slices precooked bacon (such as Jimmy Dean)
8 (1-ounce) slices of 100% whole wheat bread (such as Nature's Own Double Fiber Wheat Bread)
Butter-flavored cooking spray
4 large eggs
⅛ teaspoon salt
¼ teaspoon black pepper
1 small tomato, cut into 4 slices

1. Preheat broiler.
2. Combine mayonnaise, basil, and lemon juice in a small bowl, stirring with a whisk.
3. Heat bacon in microwave according to package directions; cut bacon slices in half. Place bread in a single layer on a large baking sheet. Broil 2 minutes on each side or until toasted.
4. Heat a large nonstick skillet over medium-high heat. Coat pan with cooking spray. Crack eggs over pan; sprinkle with salt and pepper. Cook eggs 3 minutes or until desired degree of doneness.
5. Spread mayonnaise mixture evenly on toast; top each of 4 slices toast with 1 egg, 2 bacon halves, and 1 tomato slice. Top with remaining 4 slices of toast. Cut sandwiches in half diagonally. **Yield:** 4 servings (serving size: 1 sandwich).

Per serving: CALORIES 152 (70% from fat); FAT 11.8g (saturated fat 3g); PROTEIN 8.3g; CARBOHYDRATES 2.8g; FIBER 0.4g; CHOLESTEROL 222mg; IRON 1.1mg; SODIUM 337mg; CALCIUM 32mg

Tex-Mex Breakfast Burrito

prep: 10 minutes • **cook:** 5 minutes   *POINTS* value: 6

This hearty burrito filled with scrambled egg substitute, avocado, and cheese will keep you satisfied all morning. For a different variation, try Southwestern or chive-seasoned egg substitute.

  1   cup egg substitute
  ¼   teaspoon salt
  ¼   teaspoon black pepper
  2   teaspoons butter
Cooking spray
  4   (7½-inch) 96% fat-free whole wheat tortillas
  ½   cup refrigerated fresh salsa
  ½   avocado, peeled and diced
  6   tablespoons reduced-fat sour cream
  ¼   cup (1-ounce) reduced-fat shredded Cheddar cheese
  2   green onions, thinly sliced
Chopped fresh cilantro and fresh lime juice (optional)

1. Combine egg substitute, salt, and pepper in a medium bowl, stirring with a whisk. Melt butter in a nonstick skillet coated with cooking spray over medium-high heat. Add egg mixture to pan; cook 2 minutes or until eggs are soft-scrambled, stirring frequently. Remove from pan; keep warm.

2. Heat tortillas according to package directions. Top each tortilla evenly with egg mixture, salsa, avocado, sour cream, cheese, and green onions. Sprinkle with cilantro, and drizzle with lime juice, if desired. Roll up tortillas. **Yield:** 4 servings (serving size: 1 burrito).

Per serving: CALORIES 276 (37% from fat); FAT 11.4g (saturated fat 3.2g); PROTEIN 14g; CARBOHYDRATES 29.2g; FIBER 4.5g; CHOLESTEROL 11mg; IRON 1.7mg; SODIUM 749mg; CALCIUM 93mg

Menu
POINTS value
per serving: 7

Tex-Mex Breakfast Burrito

1 Orange
POINTS value: 1

Game Plan

1. Prepare eggs.

2. Slice green onions, dice avocado, chop cilantro, and heat tortillas.

3. Assemble burritos.

Menu
POINTS value
per serving: 6

Country Omelet Wrap

Mexican Hot Chocolate

Game Plan

1. Chop ham and vegetables.

2. While vegetable mixture cooks:
• Prepare eggs.

3. While omelet cooks:
• Prepare Mexican Hot Chocolate.

Country Omelet Wrap

prep: 5 minutes • **cook:** 8 minutes   **POINTS** value: 4

In this savory breakfast wrap, we were able to keep the flavor and texture of a traditional omelet yet cut the cholesterol and fat in half by combining a whole egg with egg whites.

Cooking spray
  1 (1-ounce) slice 33%-less-sodium ham (such as Boar's Head Lower Sodium Ham), chopped
 ⅓ cup finely chopped onion
 ¼ cup finely chopped green bell pepper
 ¼ cup finely chopped tomato
  4 egg whites
  1 large egg
 ⅛ teaspoon salt
 ⅛ teaspoon freshly ground black pepper
 ¼ cup (1-ounce) preshredded reduced-fat Mexican 4-cheese blend
  1 (12-inch) multi-grain sandwich wrap (such as Flatout)
  2 tablespoons fat-free black bean and corn salsa (such as Muir Glen Organic)
  4 teaspoons fat-free sour cream

1. Heat a large nonstick skillet over medium-high heat. Coat pan with cooking spray. Add ham and next 3 ingredients to pan; cook 3 minutes, stirring occasionally, or until vegetables are crisp-tender.
2. While vegetable mixture cooks, combine egg whites and the next 3 ingredients in a medium bowl, stirring with a whisk.
3. Add egg mixture to pan. Cook until edges begin to set (about 2 minutes). Gently lift edges of omelet with a spatula, and tilt pan so uncooked portion flows underneath. Cook 2 to 3 minutes or until center is just set. Sprinkle omelet with cheese. Cook 1 minute or until cheese melts. Loosen omelet carefully with a spatula.
4. Carefully slide omelet out of pan onto wrap. Starting at short end, roll up wrap; cut in half. Top each half evenly with salsa and sour cream. **Yield:** 2 servings (serving size: ½ omelet wrap, 1 tablespoon salsa, and 2 teaspoons sour cream).

Per serving: CALORIES 208 (28% from fat); FAT 6.5g (saturated fat 2.3g); PROTEIN 23.3g; CARBOHYDRATES 17.2g; FIBER 5.2g; CHOLESTEROL 119mg; IRON 1.7mg; SODIUM 772mg; CALCIUM 160mg

Mexican Hot Chocolate

prep: 1 minute • **cook:** 3 minutes   **POINTS** value: 2

Bring 1½ cups fat-free milk to a simmer in a medium saucepan. Remove pan from heat. Stir in 2 (.29-ounce) envelopes fat-free hot cocoa mix (such as Swiss Miss Sensible Sweets), ¼ teaspoon instant coffee granules, and ⅛ teaspoon ground cinnamon. **Yield:** 2 servings (serving size: ¾ cup).

Per serving: CALORIES 100 (1% from fat); FAT 0.1g (saturated fat 0g); PROTEIN 9.4g; CARBOHYDRATES 14.4g; FIBER 0.5g; CHOLESTEROL 4mg; IRON 0.1mg; SODIUM 170mg; CALCIUM 335mg

Fish & Shellfish

Menu
POINTS value
per serving: 8

Grouper with Cilantro Pesto

Sliced Tomatoes with
Cilantro Mayonnaise

Game Plan

1. While grill heats:
- Prepare cilantro pesto and mayonnaise.
- Prepare fish for grilling.

2. While fish cooks:
- Slice tomatoes.

Grouper with Cilantro Pesto

prep: 9 minutes • **cook:** 8 minutes   *POINTS* value: 6

Cilantro is used in the pesto instead of the traditional basil to give this lively green sauce a hint of citruslike flavor. In this menu, the pesto pulls double duty as a topping for grilled fish and as a stir-in ingredient to dress up the mayonnaise for the tomatoes.

  1½   cups packed cilantro leaves
   3   garlic cloves
   2   tablespoons pine nuts
  ⅓   cup preshredded fresh Parmesan cheese
  ¼   teaspoon salt, divided
  ¼   teaspoon black pepper, divided
   2   tablespoons olive oil, divided
   2   tablespoons fresh lemon juice
   4   (6-ounce) grouper fillets
Cooking spray

1. Prepare grill.
2. Place first 4 ingredients, ⅛ teaspoon salt, and ⅛ teaspoon pepper in a food processor; process until chopped. With processor on, slowly pour 1½ tablespoons oil through food chute; process until well blended. Remove pesto from food processor bowl; set aside 1½ teaspoons pesto for Cilantro Mayonnaise (see recipe below).
3. Combine remaining ½ tablespoon oil and lemon juice; brush over grouper fillets. Sprinkle fillets with remaining ⅛ teaspoon salt and pepper.
4. Place grouper on grill rack coated with cooking spray; grill 4 to 5 minutes on each side or until fish flakes easily when tested with a fork. Serve with pesto.
Yield: 4 servings (serving size: 1 fillet and about 1¾ tablespoons cilantro pesto).

Per serving: CALORIES 273 (42% from fat); FAT 12.8g (saturated fat 2.6g); PROTEIN 36.2g; CARBOHYDRATES 2.4g; FIBER 0.4g; CHOLESTEROL 67mg; IRON 1.9mg; SODIUM 475mg; CALCIUM 133mg

Sliced Tomatoes with Cilantro Mayonnaise

prep: 2 minutes   *POINTS* value: 2

Combine ¼ cup light mayonnaise and 1½ teaspoons Cilantro Pesto (see recipe above). Slice 2 medium tomatoes. To serve, spoon cilantro mayonnaise over sliced tomatoes. **Yield:** 4 servings (serving size: 2 slices tomato and 1 tablespoon cilantro mayonnaise).

Per serving: CALORIES 68 (75% from fat); FAT 5.7g (saturated fat 0.9g); PROTEIN 0.9g; CARBOHYDRATES 3.8g; FIBER 0.8g; CHOLESTEROL 6mg; IRON 0.2mg; SODIUM 145mg; CALCIUM 13mg

Fish in Coconut, Ginger, and Pineapple Broth

prep: 7 minutes • **cook:** 14 minutes

POINTS value: 4

Reminiscent of a Thai fish soup, this dish gets a flavor boost from fresh basil and green onions. Gently poaching mild grouper preserves its delicate texture and adds depth to the creamy broth.

  4 (6-ounce) grouper fillets
  2 teaspoons salt-free Thai seasoning (such as Frontier)
  ¼ teaspoon salt
  1 (8-ounce) can pineapple tidbits in juice, divided
  ½ cup fat-free, less-sodium chicken broth
  6 (⅛-inch-thick) slices unpeeled fresh ginger
  ½ cup light coconut milk
  2 teaspoons low-sodium soy sauce
  2 tablespoons sliced green onions
  2 tablespoons chopped fresh basil

1. Sprinkle fish with Thai seasoning and salt.
2. Drain pineapple juice over a large nonstick skillet; reserve pineapple tidbits for Pineapple Rice (see recipe below). Add broth and ginger to pineapple juice in pan; cover and bring to a boil. Stir in coconut milk and soy sauce; reduce heat to a simmer. Place fish fillets in pan in a single layer. Cover; simmer 10 minutes or until fish flakes easily when tested with a fork. Discard ginger.
3. To serve, spoon fish and broth evenly over Pineapple Rice. Sprinkle evenly with green onions and basil. **Yield:** 4 servings (serving size: 1 fillet and about ⅓ cup broth mixture).

Per serving: CALORIES 191 (16% from fat); FAT 3.3g (saturated fat 1.8g); PROTEIN 34.1g; CARBOHYDRATES 4.8g; FIBER 0.2g; CHOLESTEROL 63mg; IRON 1.8mg; SODIUM 416mg; CALCIUM 53mg

Pineapple Rice

prep: 2 minutes • **cook:** 3 minutes • **other:** 1 minute

POINTS value: 2

Microwave 1 (10-ounce) package frozen brown rice according to package directions. Pour rice into a small bowl. Stir in reserved pineapple tidbits from Fish in Coconut, Ginger, and Pineapple Broth (see recipe above) and 3 tablespoons chopped green onions. **Yield:** 4 servings (serving size: about ½ cup).

Per serving: CALORIES 102 (5% from fat); FAT 0.6g (saturated fat 0.1g); PROTEIN 2.3g; CARBOHYDRATES 22.3g; FIBER 1.5g; CHOLESTEROL 0mg; IRON 0.2mg; SODIUM 4mg; CALCIUM 19mg

Menu
POINTS value
per serving: 6

Fish in Coconut, Ginger, and Pineapple Broth

Pineapple Rice

Game Plan
1. Season fish.

2. While broth for fish comes to a boil:
  • Chop green onions and basil.

3. While fish cooks:
  • Prepare rice.

Menu
POINTS value
per serving: 7

Almond-Crusted Flounder

Broiled Asparagus

½ cup precooked brown rice
POINTS value: 2

Game Plan

1. While broiler preheats:
 • Prepare almond coating for flounder.

2. Season fish with almond coating, and prepare asparagus on baking sheet.

Almond-Crusted Flounder

prep: 8 minutes • **cook:** 8 minutes   **POINTS** value: 4

Use the same pan to broil the flounder and asparagus to make this a superfast meal with easy cleanup.

- ¼ cup slivered almonds
- ¼ cup firmly packed fresh parsley
- 1 large shallot, sliced
- 2 garlic cloves
- 1 tablespoon Italian breadcrumbs
- 2 tablespoons fresh lemon juice
- 4 (6-ounce) flounder or other firm white fish fillets
- ¼ teaspoon salt
- ¼ teaspoon black pepper
- Cooking spray
- Lemon wedges (optional)

1. Preheat broiler.
2. Place almonds and next 3 ingredients in a food processor; process until finely chopped. Add breadcrumbs and lemon juice; process until well combined. Sprinkle fillets with salt and pepper. Rub almond mixture over fillets, and spray with cooking spray. Place fillets on half of a rimmed baking sheet coated with cooking spray, reserving other half of pan for Broiled Asparagus (see recipe below). Broil 8 to 10 minutes or until fish flakes easily when tested with a fork. Serve with lemon wedges, if desired. **Yield:** 4 servings (serving size: 1 fillet).

Per serving: CALORIES 206 (23% from fat); FAT 5.2g (saturated fat 0.8g); PROTEIN 33.9g; CARBOHYDRATES 4.7g; FIBER 1g; CHOLESTEROL 82mg; IRON 1.3mg; SODIUM 314mg; CALCIUM 59mg

Broiled Asparagus

prep: 2 minutes • **cook:** 8 minutes   **POINTS** value: 1

Add 1 pound of asparagus, trimmed, to reserved half of baking sheet from Almond-Crusted Flounder (see recipe above). Drizzle with 2 tablespoons lemon juice and 2 teaspoons olive oil; sprinkle with ⅛ teaspoon salt and ¼ teaspoon black pepper. Broil 8 to 10 minutes or until tender. **Yield:** 4 servings (serving size: about ¼ of asparagus).

Per serving: CALORIES 51 (44% from fat); FAT 2.5g (saturated fat 0.4g); PROTEIN 2.5g; CARBOHYDRATES 5.1g; FIBER 2.4g; CHOLESTEROL 0mg; IRON 2.4mg; SODIUM 61mg; CALCIUM 28mg

Dilled Salmon Cakes with Tzatziki Sauce

prep: 7 minutes • **cook:** 7 minutes   ***POINTS*** value: 4

Tzatziki is a traditional Greek sauce made with yogurt, cucumbers, and lemon. Its tangy flavor pairs perfectly with the warm, tender salmon cakes. Try serving this salmon on a white wheat hamburger bun topped with lettuce leaves and a slice of tomato for a quick sandwich with a *POINTS* value of 4.

2	(6-ounce) cans skinless, boneless pink salmon in water (such as Bumble Bee), drained
⅓	cup dry breadcrumbs
3	tablespoons chopped green onions
1	tablespoon chopped fresh dill
1	large egg
⅛	teaspoon black pepper
2	teaspoons canola oil
¼	cup plain low-fat yogurt
¼	cup grated peeled seeded cucumber
½	teaspoon grated lemon rind
⅛	teaspoon salt

1. Combine first 6 ingredients in a medium bowl. Shape mixture into 4 (½-inch-thick) patties.
2. Heat oil in a large skillet over medium-high heat. Add salmon patties to pan; cook 3 to 4 minutes on each side or until browned.
3. While patties cook, combine yogurt and remaining ingredients. To serve, spoon cucumber sauce over salmon cakes. **Yield:** 2 servings (serving size: 2 salmon cakes and about ¼ cup sauce).

Per serving: CALORIES 176 (55% from fat); FAT 10.8g (saturated fat 1.6g); PROTEIN 31.2g; CARBOHYDRATES 16.6g; FIBER 1.4g; CHOLESTEROL 151mg; IRON 1.6mg; SODIUM 664mg; CALCIUM 114mg

Cucumber and Cherry Tomato Salad

prep: 5 minutes   ***POINTS*** value: 1

Combine ½ pint halved cherry tomatoes, 1 cup sliced cucumber, and ¼ cup halved and thinly sliced sweet onion in a medium bowl. Combine 1 tablespoon balsamic vinegar, ½ teaspoon sugar, ½ teaspoon extra-virgin olive oil, ⅛ teaspoon salt, and ⅛ teaspoon freshly ground black pepper in a small bowl; stir with a whisk. Pour dressing over salad; toss well. **Yield:** 2 servings (serving size: about 1 cup).

Per serving: CALORIES 50 (27% from fat); FAT 1.5g (saturated fat 0.2g); PROTEIN 1.2g; CARBOHYDRATES 8.7g; FIBER 1.5g; CHOLESTEROL 0mg; IRON 0.6mg; SODIUM 156mg; CALCIUM 17mg

Menu
POINTS value
per serving: 5

**Dilled Salmon Cakes
with Tzatziki Sauce**

**Cucumber and
Cherry Tomato Salad**

Game Plan

1. Chop vegetables for salmon patties and salad.

2. Chop dill, and prepare patties.

3. While patties cook:
  • Prepare cucumber sauce.
  • Prepare salad.

Game Plan

1. While broiler preheats:
   • Prepare miso glaze.
   • Mince ginger.

2. While salmon cooks:
   • Prepare spinach.

Miso-Glazed Salmon

prep: 5 minutes • **cook:** 8 minutes   *POINTS* value: 6

The salty-sweet seasoning from miso, a fermented soybean paste that is commonly used in Japanese cuisine, stands up well to rich salmon. Look for miso in the refrigerated produce section of your supermarket. It will keep up to 2 months when refrigerated in an airtight container. Use leftover miso as a thick rub for meat, chicken thighs, and tofu.

  3   tablespoons white miso paste
  1   teaspoon grated orange rind
  2   tablespoons fresh orange juice
  1   teaspoon low-sodium soy sauce
  1   teaspoon sugar
  4   (6-ounce) salmon fillets (about 1 to 1½ inches thick)
Cooking spray

1. Preheat broiler.
2. Combine miso paste and next 4 ingredients in a medium bowl, stirring with a whisk. Place fillets on rack of broiler pan coated with cooking spray. Spread miso mixture on each fillet. Broil 8 minutes or until fish flakes easily when tested with a fork. **Yield:** 4 servings (serving size: 1 fillet).

Per serving: CALORIES 278 (30% from fat); FAT 9.5g (saturated fat 1.5g); PROTEIN 40.8g; CARBOHYDRATES 8.7g; FIBER 2.3g; CHOLESTEROL 99mg; IRON 1.8mg; SODIUM 554mg; CALCIUM 10mg

Spinach with Ginger

prep: 4 minutes • **cook:** 6 minutes   *POINTS* value: 1

Heat 2 teaspoons canola oil in a large skillet over medium-high heat. Add 2 tablespoons minced peeled fresh ginger, and sauté 1 minute or until softened. Add 2 (10-ounce) packages fresh spinach, in batches, and cook, stirring constantly, 5 minutes or until spinach wilts. Stir in ¼ teaspoon salt. **Yield:** 4 servings (serving size: ¾ cup).

Per serving: CALORIES 56 (47% from fat); FAT 2.9g (saturated fat 0.3g); PROTEIN 4.1g; CARBOHYDRATES 5.7g; FIBER 3.2g; CHOLESTEROL 0mg; IRON 3.9mg; SODIUM 258mg; CALCIUM 141mg

pictured on page 37

Salmon with Tomatoes and Citrus

prep: 9 minutes • **cook:** 10 minutes

POINTS value: 6

The subtle sweetness from the fresh lemon and orange juices balances the acidity of the tomato in the salsa. You can purchase pretoasted sesame seeds at the supermarket. To toast them yourself, heat the sesame seeds in a dry skillet over medium-high heat, stirring frequently for 1 to 2 minutes or until they become golden.

- 4 (6-ounce) salmon fillets (about 1½ inches thick)
- ¼ teaspoon salt
- ¼ teaspoon black pepper
- 1 teaspoon olive oil
- Cooking spray
- 1 cup chopped plum tomato
- ½ cup chopped red onion
- 1 teaspoon grated orange rind
- 1 teaspoon grated lemon rind
- ¼ cup fresh orange juice
- ¼ cup fresh lemon juice
- 4 lemon wedges

1. Sprinkle salmon with salt and pepper. Heat oil in a large nonstick skillet over medium-high heat. Coat pan and salmon with cooking spray. Add salmon to pan; cook 4 to 5 minutes on each side or until salmon is browned and flakes easily when tested with a fork.

2. While salmon cooks, combine tomato and remaining ingredients. Spoon tomato mixture over salmon, and serve with lemon wedges. **Yield:** 4 servings (serving size: 1 salmon fillet and about ⅓ cup tomato mixture).

Per serving: CALORIES 285 (34% from fat); FAT 10.8g (saturated fat 1.7g); PROTEIN 39.2g; CARBOHYDRATES 9g; FIBER 1.1g; CHOLESTEROL 99mg; IRON 1.2mg; SODIUM 247mg; CALCIUM 22mg

Sesame-Lime Brown Rice

prep: 3 minutes • **cook:** 1 minute, 30 seconds

POINTS value: 2

Microwave 1 (8.8-ounce) package precooked brown rice (such as Uncle Ben's Ready Rice) according to package directions. Pour rice into a small bowl. Stir in 1 tablespoon toasted sesame seeds, ½ teaspoon grated lime rind, 2 tablespoons fresh lime juice, ½ teaspoon dark sesame oil, and ¼ teaspoon salt. **Yield:** 4 servings (serving size: about ½ cup).

Per serving: CALORIES 120 (26% from fat); FAT 3.5g (saturated fat 0.5g); PROTEIN 2.7g; CARBOHYDRATES 20.3g; FIBER 1.4g; CHOLESTEROL 0mg; IRON 0.7mg; SODIUM 148mg; CALCIUM 26mg

Game Plan

1. While broiler preheats:
  • Zest, slice, and quarter lemons.
  • Assemble fish on broiler pan.

2. While fish cooks:
  • Prepare green beans.

Bay-Scented Snapper with Lemon

prep: 6 minutes • **cook:** 9 minutes   **POINTS** value: 4

The seasoning combination of lemon and bay leaves makes versatile snapper simply delicious. Substitute tilapia or flounder for the snapper, if desired.

    1   teaspoon grated lemon rind
    1   tablespoon olive oil
    4   (6-ounce) red snapper fillets
    ¼   teaspoon salt
    ¼   teaspoon freshly ground black pepper
  Cooking spray
    8   fresh bay leaves
    8   lemon slices
    4   lemon wedges

1. Preheat broiler.
2. Combine lemon rind and oil in a small bowl; set aside.
3. Sprinkle fillets with salt and pepper. Place fish on broiler pan coated with cooking spray. Drizzle lemon mixture over fish. Arrange 2 bay leaves on each fillet. Top with 2 lemon slices. Broil 9 to 10 minutes or until fish flakes easily when tested with a fork. Serve with lemon wedges. **Yield:** 4 servings (serving size: 1 fillet).

Per serving: CALORIES 205 (25% from fat); FAT 5.8g (saturated fat 1g); PROTEIN 35.1g; CARBOHYDRATES 1.5g; FIBER 0.5g; CHOLESTEROL 63mg; IRON 0.4mg; SODIUM 255mg; CALCIUM 59mg

French Green Beans with Tomatoes and Tarragon

prep: 4 minutes • **cook:** 3 minutes   **POINTS** value: 1

Pierce bag of 1 (8-ounce) package pretrimmed French-style green beans with a fork. Microwave at HIGH 3 minutes or until tender. Place beans and 1 quartered and sliced plum tomato in a large bowl. Combine 1 tablespoon fresh lemon juice, 1 tablespoon olive oil, 2 teaspoons chopped fresh tarragon, ¼ teaspoon salt, and ¼ teaspoon freshly ground black pepper in a small bowl; stir with a whisk. Pour dressing over beans and tomato; toss gently to coat. **Yield:** 4 servings (serving size: ¾ cup).

Per serving: CALORIES 58 (56% from fat); FAT 3.6g (saturated fat 0.5g); PROTEIN 0.9g; CARBOHYDRATES 4.4g; FIBER 1.6g; CHOLESTEROL 0mg; IRON 0.3mg; SODIUM 146mg; CALCIUM 31mg

Grilled Citrus-Basil Snapper

prep: 4 minutes • **cook:** 5 minutes   *POINTS* value: 4

A Microplane® grater is an excellent kitchen tool to use for finely zesting oranges, limes, and lemons. It's fast and efficient, and it removes the intensely flavored rind without any of the bitter white pith. As an alternative, you can also use a zester or a handheld grater.

⅓   cup orange juice
1   teaspoon lime zest
¼   cup fresh lime juice
½   teaspoon kosher salt
½   teaspoon freshly ground black pepper
4   (6-ounce) snapper or other firm white fish fillets
Cooking spray
2   tablespoons chopped fresh basil

1. Prepare grill.
2. Combine first 5 ingredients in a small bowl. Place fish in a shallow dish; drizzle orange juice mixture over fish.
3. Place fish on a grill rack coated with cooking spray. Grill fish 5 minutes or until fish flakes easily when tested with a fork, turning once after 3 minutes. Baste fish occasionally with orange juice mixture while grilling. Sprinkle with basil, and serve immediately. **Yield:** 4 servings (serving size: 1 fillet).

Per serving: CALORIES 187 (12% from fat); FAT 2.4g (saturated fat 0.5g); PROTEIN 35.2g; CARBOHYDRATES 4.5g; FIBER 0.5g; CHOLESTEROL 63mg; IRON 0.5mg; SODIUM 345mg; CALCIUM 64mg

Sautéed Spinach with Goat Cheese and Pine Nuts

prep: 1 minute • **cook:** 5 minutes   *POINTS* value: 2

Heat a large nonstick skillet over medium-high heat. Coat pan with cooking spray. Add 2 (6-ounce) packages fresh baby spinach to pan; cook 2 minutes, stirring often. Stir in ¼ teaspoon kosher salt and ¼ teaspoon freshly ground black pepper. Cook 2 to 3 minutes or until spinach is wilted, stirring often. Top with ¼ cup (1 ounce) crumbled goat cheese and 2 tablespoons toasted pine nuts. Serve immediately. **Yield:** 4 servings (serving size: about ⅓ cup).

Per serving: CALORIES 74 (59% from fat); FAT 5.4g (saturated fat 1.7g); PROTEIN 4.6g; CARBOHYDRATES 3.9g; FIBER 2.1g; CHOLESTEROL 5.6mg; IRON 2.7mg; SODIUM 221mg; CALCIUM 107mg

Menu
POINTS value
per serving: 6

Grilled Citrus-Basil Snapper

Sautéed Spinach with Goat Cheese and Pine Nuts

Game Plan

1. While grill heats:
• Prepare orange juice mixture for fish.
• Chop basil.
• Toast pine nuts.

2. While fish cooks:
• Prepare spinach.

Menu
POINTS value
per serving: 7

Tilapia with Cucumber Relish

Red Potatoes with Oregano

Game Plan

1. While broiler preheats:
   - Chop oregano and mint, and zest lemon.
   - Quarter potatoes, and prepare butter mixture.
   - Season fish.

2. While fish cooks:
   - Cook potatoes.
   - Prepare relish.

Tilapia with Cucumber Relish

prep: 7 minutes • **cook:** 7 minutes   **POINTS** value: 5

The Greek-style cucumber relish spooned over the broiled tilapia relies on mint, oregano, and feta cheese to deliver its assertive flavor. English cucumbers naturally have fewer seeds and a thinner skin than regular cucumbers. Because there's no need to seed or peel them, they can be prepared faster. Find them in most major grocery stores individually wrapped in plastic.

  1   teaspoon olive oil
  4   (6-ounce) tilapia fillets
  1   teaspoon Greek seasoning
Cooking spray
  1   cup chopped English cucumber
  ½ cup prechopped red onion
  ½ cup prechopped tricolor bell pepper mix
  2   tablespoons chopped fresh oregano
1½ tablespoons chopped fresh mint
  2   tablespoons orange juice
  2   teaspoons white wine vinegar
  1   teaspoon honey
  ⅛ teaspoon salt
  ⅛ teaspoon black pepper
  ½ cup (2 ounces) crumbled feta cheese

1. Preheat broiler.
2. Brush olive oil evenly over fish; sprinkle with Greek seasoning. Place fish on the rack of a broiler pan coated with cooking spray. Broil 5 inches from heat 7 minutes or until fish flakes easily when tested with a fork.
3. While fish cooks, combine cucumber and remaining 10 ingredients in a small bowl; toss well. To serve, spoon relish evenly over each fish fillet. **Yield:** 4 servings (serving size: 1 fillet and ½ cup relish).

Per serving: CALORIES 237 (27% from fat); FAT 7.2g (saturated fat 3.3g); PROTEIN 36.9g; CARBOHYDRATES 6.7g; FIBER 1g; CHOLESTEROL 98mg; IRON 1.3mg; SODIUM 342mg; CALCIUM 109mg

Red Potatoes with Oregano

prep: 5 minutes • **cook:** 8 minutes   **POINTS** value: 2

Place ¾ pound small red potatoes, quartered, in a medium saucepan, and cover with water. Bring to a boil. Reduce heat, and simmer 6 minutes or until tender. Drain. Combine 1 tablespoon melted butter, 2 teaspoons grated lemon rind, 1½ teaspoons chopped fresh oregano, ½ teaspoon salt, ¼ teaspoon garlic powder, and ⅛ teaspoon crushed red pepper in a medium bowl; stir with a whisk. Add cooked potatoes; toss gently to coat. **Yield:** 4 servings (serving size: ½ cup).

Per serving: CALORIES 106 (45% from fat); FAT 5.3g (saturated fat 2.2g); PROTEIN 1.7g; CARBOHYDRATES 13.9g; FIBER 1.6g; CHOLESTEROL 8mg; IRON 0.6mg; SODIUM 316mg; CALCIUM 13mg

Banana–Whole Wheat Pancakes
with Strawberry Syrup | page 13

Berry and Granola Greek Yogurt
Parfaits | page 9

Smoked Salmon–Spinach
Omelet | page 18

35

Crispy Curry Scallops | page 57

Salmon with Tomatoes and Citrus | page 29

Pecan-Crusted Tilapia | page 49

**Spice-Rubbed Shrimp Soft Tacos
with Red Salsa** | page 55

Pasta with Butternut Squash, Fried Rosemary, and Parmesan | page 66

Grilled Vegetable
Napoleons | page 62

Beef Fillets with Cranberry-Wine Sauce | page 76

Jerk-Seasoned Pork Tenderloin | page 88

Ginger-Teriyaki Strip Steaks | page 75

Beef and Pepperoni Pizza | page 70

Ginger-Sesame Pork Chops | page 84

Chicken with Pine Nut Gremolata | page 92

**Chicken Cutlets with Fontina
and Fresh Blueberry Sauce** | page 96

48

pictured on page 38

Pecan-Crusted Tilapia

prep: 6 minutes • **cook:** 13 minutes   ***POINTS*** value: 6

If you have a minichopper, use it to finely chop the pecans. Otherwise, take the time to use a large chef's knife to finely chop the pecans before dredging the fish.

- 2 teaspoons light mayonnaise
- 2 teaspoons Dijon mustard
- 4 (6-ounce) tilapia fillets
- ½ teaspoon salt
- ¼ teaspoon black pepper
- ½ cup all-purpose flour
- ⅓ cup finely chopped pecans
- 1 tablespoon olive oil
- Cooking spray
- 4 lemon wedges

1. Combine mayonnaise and mustard in a small bowl. Sprinkle fish with salt and pepper.
2. Combine flour and pecans in a shallow dish. Brush both sides of fish with mayonnaise mixture; dredge in pecan mixture. Discard any remaining pecan mixture.
3. Heat oil in a large nonstick skillet coated with cooking spray over medium-high heat. Add fish to pan. Cook, in 2 batches, 3 minutes on each side or until fish flakes easily when tested with a fork. Serve with lemon wedges. **Yield:** 4 servings (serving size: 1 fillet).

Per serving: CALORIES 271 (34% from fat); FAT 10.3g (saturated fat 1.9g); PROTEIN 35.6g; CARBOHYDRATES 9.3g; FIBER 0.7g; CHOLESTEROL 86mg; IRON 1.6mg; SODIUM 459mg; CALCIUM 22mg

Cranberry Coleslaw

prep: 3 minutes   ***POINTS*** value: 2

Combine 2 tablespoons cider vinegar, 1 tablespoon sugar, 2 teaspoons olive oil, and ½ teaspoon salt in a small bowl; stir with a whisk. Combine 4 cups shredded coleslaw and ½ cup sweetened dried cranberries in a large bowl. Pour dressing over slaw; toss gently to coat. **Yield:** 4 servings (serving size: about ¾ cup).

Per serving: CALORIES 92 (24% from fat); FAT 2.5g (saturated fat 0.4g); PROTEIN 0.5g; CARBOHYDRATES 18.2g; FIBER 1.9g; CHOLESTEROL 0mg; IRON 0.3mg; SODIUM 300mg; CALCIUM 22mg

---

Menu
POINTS value
per serving: 8

Pecan-Crusted Tilapia

Cranberry Coleslaw

Game Plan

1. Measure and combine ingredients for slaw.

2. Prepare coating for fish.

3. While fish cooks:
- Toss slaw.

Menu
POINTS value
per serving: 5

Fennel-Crusted Tuna

Fennel and Parsley Salad

Game Plan

1. Measure and prepare ingredients
for salad.

2. Crush fennel seeds, and season
tuna.

3. While tuna cooks:
• Toss salad.

Fennel-Crusted Tuna

prep: 4 minutes • **cook:** 5 minutes   *POINTS* value: 4

**To quickly crush fennel seeds, place them in a small zip-top plastic
bag. Wrap the plastic bag in a thin kitchen towel, and, using a flat-
sided meat mallet or a rolling pin, pound the seeds until they are
crushed.**

> 1   teaspoon olive oil
> 4   (6-ounce) tuna steaks (about ¾ inch thick)
> 1   teaspoon fennel seeds, crushed
> ½   teaspoon salt

1. Heat oil in a large skillet over medium heat. Sprinkle both sides of tuna steaks
evenly with fennel seeds and salt. Add tuna to pan; cook 2 minutes on each side or
to desired degree of doneness. **Yield:** 4 servings (serving size: 1 tuna steak).

Per serving: CALORIES 195 (13% from fat); FAT 2.9g (saturated fat 0.6g); PROTEIN 39.9g; CARBOHYDRATES 0.3g; FIBER 0.2g; CHOLESTEROL 77mg; IRON 1.3mg; SODIUM 354mg; CALCIUM 33mg

Fennel and Parsley Salad

prep: 9 minutes   *POINTS* value: 1

Combine ½ teaspoon lemon rind, 1 tablespoon fresh lemon juice, 2 teaspoons olive
oil, ¼ teaspoon salt, and ⅛ teaspoon freshly ground black pepper in a small bowl;
stir with a whisk. Combine 3 cups thinly sliced fennel bulb (about 1 medium bulb)
and 1 cup fresh flat-leaf parsley leaves in a medium bowl. Pour dressing over salad;
toss gently to coat. **Yield:** 4 servings (serving size: ¾ cup).

Per serving: CALORIES 47 (50% from fat); FAT 2.6g (saturated fat 0.4g); PROTEIN 1.3g; CARBOHYDRATES 6.1g; FIBER 2.6g; CHOLESTEROL 0mg; IRON 1.4mg; SODIUM 188mg; CALCIUM 54mg

Tuna with Orange–Green Onion Vinaigrette

prep: 5 minutes • **cook:** 5 minutes   *POINTS* value: 5

This vinaigrette drizzled over seared tuna steaks capitalizes on a few high-flavor ingredients, such as orange marmalade, green onions, and rice vinegar.

2	tablespoons orange juice
2	tablespoons low-sugar orange marmalade
2	tablespoons thinly sliced green onions
1	tablespoon rice vinegar
⅛	teaspoon salt

Pinch ground red pepper

2	teaspoons canola oil, divided
4	(6-ounce) tuna steaks
2	teaspoons sesame seeds
¼	teaspoon salt

1. Combine first 6 ingredients in a small bowl; stir with a whisk. Stir in 1 teaspoon oil; set aside.

2. Heat remaining 1 teaspoon oil in a large nonstick skillet over medium-high heat. Sprinkle both sides of tuna evenly with sesame seeds and ¼ teaspoon salt. Add tuna to pan; cook 2 minutes on each side or until desired degree of doneness. To serve, drizzle vinaigrette over tuna. **Yield:** 4 servings (serving size: 1 tuna steak and 1½ tablespoons vinaigrette).

Per serving: CALORIES 229 (18% from fat); FAT 4.6g (saturated fat 0.7g); PROTEIN 40.1g; CARBOHYDRATES 4.4g; FIBER 0.3g; CHOLESTEROL 77mg; IRON 1.4mg; SODIUM 282mg; CALCIUM 32mg

Sesame Steamed Vegetables

prep: 2 minutes • **cook:** 7 minutes   *POINTS* value: 1

Microwave 1 (16-ounce) package frozen California-blend vegetable mixture (broccoli, cauliflower, and carrots) according to package directions. Pour cooked vegetables into a medium bowl. Combine 2 teaspoons reduced-sodium soy sauce and 1 teaspoon dark sesame oil in a small bowl; drizzle over vegetables. Toss gently to coat. **Yield:** 4 servings (serving size: about ¾ cup).

Per serving: CALORIES 51 (19% from fat); FAT 1.1g (saturated fat 0.2g); PROTEIN 1.5g; CARBOHYDRATES 6.7g; FIBER 2.6g; CHOLESTEROL 0mg; IRON 0mg; SODIUM 146mg; CALCIUM 0mg

Menu
POINTS value
per serving: 6

Tuna with Orange–Green Onion Vinaigrette

Sesame Steamed Vegetables

Game Plan

1. Prepare vinaigrette for tuna.

2. While vegetables cook:
  • Cook tuna.

3. While tuna cooks:
  • Toss vegetables.

Ginger-Garlic Shrimp

prep: 3 minutes • **cook:** 3 minutes   *POINTS* value: 5

Three words describe this dish: quick, easy, and tasty. Fresh ginger adds a spicy note to the shrimp, while the Asian-inspired slaw adds vibrant color.

1½	pounds peeled and deveined medium shrimp
2	teaspoons canola oil
1	teaspoon grated fresh ginger
2	garlic cloves, minced
½	teaspoon salt

Cooking spray
Lime wedges

1. Place shrimp in a large bowl. Add oil and next 3 ingredients; toss gently to coat.
2. Heat a large nonstick skillet over medium-high heat. Coat pan with cooking spray. Add shrimp to pan. Cook, stirring constantly, 3 to 4 minutes or until shrimp are done. Serve with lime wedges. **Yield:** 4 servings (serving size: about 1¼ cups).

Per serving: CALORIES 204 (23% from fat); FAT 5.3g (saturated fat 0.7g); PROTEIN 34.7g; CARBOHYDRATES 2.1g; FIBER 0.1g; CHOLESTEROL 259mg; IRON 4.1mg; SODIUM 543mg; CALCIUM 91mg

Sesame Slaw

prep: 9 minutes   *POINTS* value: 0

Combine 2 tablespoons low-sodium soy sauce, 1 tablespoon fresh lime juice, ½ teaspoon sugar, and ½ teaspoon dark sesame oil in a small bowl; stir with a whisk. Combine 2 cups thinly sliced red cabbage (about ½ small head), ¾ cup shredded carrot (1 medium), and 1¼ cups shredded zucchini (1 medium) in a medium bowl. Pour dressing over slaw; toss gently to coat. **Yield:** 4 servings (serving size: ¾ cup).

Per serving: CALORIES 38 (19% from fat); FAT 0.8g (saturated fat 0.1g); PROTEIN 1.8g; CARBOHYDRATES 7g; FIBER 1.7g; CHOLESTEROL 0mg; IRON 0.5mg; SODIUM 327mg; CALCIUM 29mg

Lemon-Basil Shrimp with Fettuccine

prep: 6 minutes • **cook:** 11 minutes   *POINTS* value: 5

This hearty pasta dish features swirls of tender fettuccine and plump shrimp tossed in a zesty tomato sauce. Top with pungent freshly grated Parmesan cheese just before serving.

    2   teaspoons olive oil
 1¼   cups vertically sliced onion
    2   garlic cloves, minced
    ½   cup dry white wine
    1   pound peeled and deveined medium shrimp
    1   (14.5-ounce) can diced tomatoes with basil, garlic, and oregano, undrained
 1½   tablespoons chopped fresh basil
    1   teaspoon grated lemon rind
    2   tablespoons fresh lemon juice
    ⅛   teaspoon black pepper
    1   (9-ounce) package refrigerated fettuccine
    ¼   cup freshly grated Parmesan cheese

1. Heat oil in a large nonstick skillet over medium heat. Add onion and garlic to pan; sauté 3 minutes or until tender. Increase heat to high; add wine. Cook 1 to 2 minutes or until wine reduces by half. Add shrimp, tomatoes, and next 4 ingredients; cook 5 minutes or until shrimp are done.
2. While shrimp cook, cook fettuccine according to package directions, omitting salt and fat. Drain.
3. Add cooked fettuccine to shrimp mixture; toss gently to coat. To serve, sprinkle evenly with Parmesan cheese. **Yield:** 6 servings (serving size: about 1 cup shrimp and pasta mixture and 2 teaspoons Parmesan cheese).

Per serving: CALORIES 269 (15% from fat); FAT 4.5g (saturated fat 1.2g); PROTEIN 20.3g; CARBOHYDRATES 32.8g; FIBER 2.7g; CHOLESTEROL 146mg; IRON 4.3mg; SODIUM 578mg; CALCIUM 148mg

Mixed Greens Salad with Parmesan

prep: 3 minutes   *POINTS* value: 1

Place 1 (5-ounce) package gourmet salad greens in a large bowl. Combine 1 tablespoon balsamic vinegar, 2 teaspoons olive oil, ⅛ teaspoon salt, and ⅛ teaspoon black pepper in a small bowl; stir with a whisk. Pour dressing over greens, and toss well. To serve, sprinkle with 1 tablespoon finely shredded fresh Parmesan cheese. **Yield:** 6 servings (serving size: 1 cup).

Per serving: CALORIES 38 (71% from fat); FAT 3g (saturated fat 1g); PROTEIN 1.9g; CARBOHYDRATES 1.4g; FIBER 0.5g; CHOLESTEROL 4mg; IRON 0.3mg; SODIUM 122mg; CALCIUM 64mg

---

Menu
POINTS value
per serving: 6

Lemon-Basil Shrimp with Fettuccine

Mixed Greens Salad with Parmesan

Game Plan

1. While water for pasta comes to a boil:
  • Prepare salad dressing.
  • Slice onion, mince garlic, and chop basil.
  • Zest and juice lemon.
  • Shred and grate cheese.

2. Cook onion, garlic, and wine mixture.

3. While shrimp mixture cooks:
  • Cook pasta.
  • Toss salad.

Menu
POINTS value
per serving: 6

Smoky Shrimp and Vegetables

Creamy Garlic-Herb Grits

Game Plan

1. Measure vegetables, and dice sausage.

2. While onion mixture cooks:
   • Bring broth to a boil for grits.

3. While shrimp mixture cooks:
   • Cook grits.

Smoky Shrimp and Vegetables

prep: 3 minutes • **cook:** 13 minutes   *POINTS* value: 4

Smoked paprika is an aromatic spice made from grinding Spanish sweet red peppers that have been cooked over wooden planks. Previously, this spice could only be purchased at specialty or gourmet stores, but it's now available in the spice section of most grocery stores. It adds a distinctive smoky taste that makes this shrimp and grits recipe memorable.

  1   teaspoon canola oil
Cooking spray
  1   cup prechopped onion
  1   cup prechopped green bell pepper
  ½   cup prechopped celery
  3   ounces smoked turkey sausage (such as Butterball), diced
  1   teaspoon bottled minced garlic
  1   (8-ounce) package prechopped tomato
  1¼ pounds peeled and deveined large shrimp
  1   teaspoon smoked paprika
  ⅛   teaspoon salt
  ⅛   teaspoon ground red pepper
  3   tablespoons dry white wine

1. Heat oil in a large nonstick skillet coated with cooking spray over medium-high heat. Add onion and next 4 ingredients to pan; sauté 3 minutes or until vegetables are tender. Add tomato; cook 1 minute. Add shrimp, paprika, salt, and red pepper. Cook 5 to 6 minutes or until shrimp are done. Stir in wine; cook 1 minute, stirring frequently. To serve, spoon shrimp mixture over Creamy Garlic-Herb Grits (see recipe below). **Yield:** 4 servings (serving size: about 1 cup shrimp mixture).

Per serving: CALORIES 188 (18% from fat); FAT 3.8g (saturated fat 1.1g); PROTEIN 26.9g; CARBOHYDRATES 9.1g; FIBER 2.2g; CHOLESTEROL 215mg; IRON 4mg; SODIUM 438mg; CALCIUM 97mg

Creamy Garlic-Herb Grits

prep: 2 minutes • **cook:** 6 minutes   *POINTS* value: 2

Bring 2 cups fat-free, less-sodium chicken broth to a boil in a medium saucepan. Add ½ cup uncooked quick-cooking grits; stir well, and return to a boil. Cover, reduce heat, and simmer 5 minutes or until thickened, stirring occasionally. Stir in ¼ cup light garlic-and-herb cheese spread (such as Alouette) and ⅓ cup sliced green onions. To serve, divide grits onto each of 4 serving plates, and top with Smoky Shrimp and Vegetables (see recipe above). Serve immediately. **Yield:** 4 servings (serving size: ½ cup).

Per serving: CALORIES 86 (24% from fat); FAT 2.3g (saturated fat 1.5g); PROTEIN 4.5g; CARBOHYDRATES 18.1g; FIBER 0.6g; CHOLESTEROL 10mg; IRON 0.9mg; SODIUM 349mg; CALCIUM 11mg

pictured on page 39

Spice-Rubbed Shrimp Soft Tacos with Red Salsa

prep: 1 minute • **cook:** 5 minutes   *POINTS* value: 8

Using preshredded cabbage and broiling the shrimp make these bold tacos an effortless and satisfying meal.

1	cup refrigerated fresh salsa
2	tablespoons chopped fresh cilantro
½	jalapeño, seeded and minced
½	tablespoon fresh lime juice
1½	pounds peeled and deveined medium shrimp
2	teaspoons ground cumin
2	teaspoons paprika
2	teaspoons canola oil
¼	teaspoon salt
¼	teaspoon freshly ground black pepper

Dash of cayenne pepper
Cooking spray

8	(6-inch) 96% fat-free heart healthy tortillas (such as Mission)
2	cups packaged angel hair slaw

1. Preheat broiler.

2. Combine salsa and next 3 ingredients in a medium bowl. Set aside.

3. Place shrimp in a large bowl. Add cumin and next 5 ingredients; toss gently to coat. Arrange shrimp in a single layer on rack of a broiler pan coated with cooking spray. Broil 5 minutes or until shrimp are done, turning once.

4. Heat tortillas according to package directions. To serve, top tortillas evenly with slaw, shrimp, and salsa. **Yield:** 4 servings (serving size: 2 tacos).

Per serving: CALORIES 419 (17% from fat); FAT 7.7g (saturated fat 0.7g); PROTEIN 39.3g; CARBOHYDRATES 40.6g; FIBER 5.5g; CHOLESTEROL 259mg; IRON 4.6mg; SODIUM 969mg; CALCIUM 100mg

Menu
POINTS value
per serving: 8

Spice-Rubbed Shrimp Soft Tacos with Red Salsa

Game Plan

1. While broiler preheats:
  • Chop cilantro and jalapeño.
  • Prepare salsa.

2. Prepare shrimp.

3. While shrimp cook:
  • Heat tortillas.

Menu
POINTS value
per serving: 8

Bayou Scallops

**Spring Greens with
Hot Sauce Dressing**

1 (1-ounce) slice French bread
POINTS value: 2

Game Plan

1. Measure and combine ingredients for salad dressing.

2. Mince garlic, slice green onions, and juice lime.

3. While scallops cook:
   • Toss salad.

Bayou Scallops

prep: 6 minutes • **cook:** 9 minutes   *POINTS* value: 5

These irresistible scallops are lightly dusted with seafood seasoning and drizzled with a garlic-lime butter sauce. Make sure to request dry-packed sea scallops at the fish counter. They tend to be fresher and haven't been soaked in water to increase their weight.

1½	pounds large sea scallops (about 12)
1	tablespoon olive oil
2	teaspoons seafood seasoning (such as Old Bay)
⅓	cup water
1	tablespoon butter
2	medium garlic cloves, minced
1	tablespoon fresh lime juice
½	cup sliced green onions

1. Pat scallops dry with paper towels. Heat oil in a large nonstick skillet over medium-high heat. Rub seafood seasoning evenly over scallops. Add scallops to pan, and cook 2 to 3 minutes on each side or until browned. Transfer scallops to a serving platter; keep warm.
2. Add water to hot pan, stirring to loosen browned bits from bottom of pan. Cook 1 to 2 minutes or until mixture is reduced by half. Add butter, stirring until it melts. Add garlic, and cook 30 seconds. Stir in lime juice and onions; cook 30 seconds. Pour sauce over scallops, and serve immediately. **Yield:** 4 servings (serving size: 3 scallops and 1 tablespoon sauce).

Per serving: CALORIES 214 (32% from fat); FAT 7.6g (saturated fat 2.4g); PROTEIN 28.7g; CARBOHYDRATES 5.8g; FIBER 0.6g; CHOLESTEROL 64mg; IRON 0.7mg; SODIUM 619mg; CALCIUM 55mg

Spring Greens with Hot Sauce Dressing

prep: 3 minutes   *POINTS* value: 1

Place 1 (5-ounce) bag mixed baby lettuces in a large bowl. Combine 1½ tablespoons extra-virgin olive oil and 2 teaspoons hot sauce in a small bowl; stir with a whisk. Stir in 1½ tablespoons drained capers. Pour dressing over lettuce, and toss well. Serve immediately. **Yield:** 4 servings (serving size: 1½ cups).

Per serving: CALORIES 52 (93% from fat); FAT 5.4g (saturated fat 0.8g); PROTEIN 0.7g; CARBOHYDRATES 1.3g; FIBER 0.9g; CHOLESTEROL 0mg; IRON 0.5mg; SODIUM 167mg; CALCIUM 21mg

pictured on page 36

Crispy Curry Scallops

prep: 5 minutes • **cook:** 5 minutes

POINTS value: 4

Panko, Japanese breadcrumbs, gives these succulent scallops a light, crispy crust. Look for panko alongside the baking ingredients at your supermarket.

1½	pounds large sea scallops (about 12)
½	cup panko (Japanese breadcrumbs)
2	teaspoons low-sodium soy sauce
1	teaspoon curry powder
2	teaspoons canola oil

Lime wedges

1. Pat scallops dry with paper towels. Place panko in a shallow dish.
2. Toss scallops with soy sauce in a medium bowl; sprinkle evenly with curry powder. Dredge in panko.
3. Heat oil in a large nonstick skillet over medium-high heat. Add scallops to pan; cook 2 to 3 minutes on each side or until browned. Serve with lime wedges.
Yield: 4 servings (serving size: 3 scallops).

Per serving: CALORIES 192 (18% from fat); FAT 3.9g (saturated fat 0.3g); PROTEIN 29.4g; CARBOHYDRATES 8g; FIBER 0.3g; CHOLESTEROL 56mg; IRON 0.7mg; SODIUM 388mg; CALCIUM 44mg

Chile-Ginger Sugar Snaps

prep: 2 minutes • **cook:** 4 minutes

POINTS value: 0

Heat a large nonstick skillet over medium-high heat. Coat pan with cooking spray. Add 1 (8-ounce) package fresh sugar snap peas, and sauté 1 minute. Combine 3 tablespoons water, ½ teaspoon grated fresh ginger, ½ teaspoon chile paste with garlic (such as sambal oelek), and ⅛ teaspoon salt in a small bowl; stir with a whisk. Add water mixture to pan, tossing to coat peas. Cook 2 minutes or until sugar snap peas are crisp-tender. **Yield:** 4 servings (serving size: ½ cup).

Per serving: CALORIES 27 (0% from fat); FAT 0g (saturated fat 0g); PROTEIN 1.3g; CARBOHYDRATES 4.7g; FIBER 1.4g; CHOLESTEROL 0mg; IRON 0.7mg; SODIUM 83mg; CALCIUM 40mg

---

Menu
POINTS value
per serving: 6

Crispy Curry Scallops

Chile-Ginger Sugar Snaps

½ **cup lemon sorbet**
POINTS value: 2

Game Plan

1. Grate ginger, and measure ingredients for sugar snaps.

2. While scallops cook:
 • Prepare sugar snaps.

Game Plan

1. Chop shallots and parsley; mince garlic, and juice lemon.
2. Prepare scallops.
3. Prepare green beans.

Scallops Piccata

prep: 6 minutes • **cook:** 9 minutes   *POINTS* value: 5

Pat the scallops dry before you sear them to remove excess moisture and ensure a nicely browned exterior. Deglazing the skillet with wine to remove the bits left behind from browning the scallops elevates the flavor of the sauce.

1½	pounds large sea scallops (about 12 scallops)
¼	teaspoon salt
¼	teaspoon black pepper
2	teaspoons olive oil
⅓	cup fresh lemon juice
3	tablespoons dry white wine
2	garlic cloves, minced
2	teaspoons capers, drained
2	tablespoons chopped fresh parsley
1	tablespoon butter

1. Pat scallops dry with paper towels; sprinkle with salt and pepper. Heat oil in a large nonstick skillet over medium-high heat. Add scallops to pan; cook 2 to 3 minutes on each side or until browned. Transfer scallops to a serving platter; keep warm.
2. Combine lemon juice and next 3 ingredients; add to hot pan, scraping pan to loosen browned bits. Cook 1 to 2 minutes or until mixture is reduced by half. Add parsley and butter; cook 1 minute or until butter melts. Pour sauce over scallops, and serve immediately. **Yield:** 4 servings (serving size: 3 scallops and about 1 tablespoon sauce).

Per serving: CALORIES 213 (27% from fat); FAT 6.5g (saturated fat 2.3g); PROTEIN 28.9g; CARBOHYDRATES 6.8g; FIBER 0.3g; CHOLESTEROL 64mg; IRON 0.7mg; SODIUM 483mg; CALCIUM 50mg

Green Beans with Shallots

prep: 4 minutes • **cook:** 6 minutes   *POINTS* value: 0

Microwave 1 (12-ounce) package pretrimmed green beans according to package directions. While green beans cook, heat a medium nonstick skillet over medium-high heat. Coat pan with cooking spray. Add 3 tablespoons chopped shallots and 2 minced garlic cloves; cook 3 minutes, stirring constantly. Add cooked green beans, ¼ teaspoon salt, and ⅛ teaspoon black pepper; cook 2 minutes or until thoroughly heated. **Yield:** 4 servings (serving size: ¾ cup).

Per serving: CALORIES 34 (3% from fat); FAT 0.1g (saturated fat 0g); PROTEIN 1.8g; CARBOHYDRATES 7.9g; FIBER 3g; CHOLESTEROL 0mg; IRON 1mg; SODIUM 152mg; CALCIUM 37mg

Meatless Main Dishes

Menu
POINTS value
per serving: 6

Black Bean Cakes

Red and Green Tomato Salad

Game Plan

1. Rinse and drain beans.

2. While rice cooks:
- Chop tomatoes, avocado, and peppers for salad.
- Mash beans, and beat eggs.

3. Prepare patties.

4. While patties cook:
- Prepare salad.

Black Bean Cakes

prep: 4 minutes • **cook:** 11 minutes • **other:** 5 minutes   *POINTS* value: 5

This summer menu capitalizes on a few pantry staples and fresh produce for a quick and inexpensive meal. The next time you cook brown rice, plan ahead and make enough rice so you'll have enough left over for this recipe.

- ½ cup water
- ½ cup instant brown rice
- 1 (15-ounce) can black beans, rinsed and drained
- ¾ cup instant brown rice
- ½ cup Italian-seasoned breadcrumbs
- 2 large eggs, lightly beaten
- ½ teaspoon garlic salt
- ½ teaspoon freshly ground black pepper
- 1 tablespoon olive oil
- ¼ cup guacamole
- ¼ cup refrigerated fresh salsa
- Reduced-fat sour cream (optional)

1. Place water in a small saucepan, cover, and bring to a boil over medium-high heat. Add rice to pan; cover, reduce heat, and simmer 5 minutes. Remove from heat; let stand 5 minutes. Fluff with a fork, and set aside.
2. Place beans in a medium bowl; mash slightly with a fork or potato masher, leaving some beans whole. Stir in reserved rice, breadcrumbs, and next 3 ingredients.
3. Divide bean mixture into 4 equal portions; shape each portion into a 1-inch-thick patty.
4. Heat oil in a large nonstick skillet over medium-high heat. Add patties to pan, and cook 4 minutes or until browned. Turn patties, and cook 2 to 3 minutes or until browned and thoroughly heated.
5. Top each of 4 cakes with 1 tablespoon guacamole and 1 tablespoon salsa. Place a dollop of sour cream on top of salsa, if desired. Serve immediately. **Yield:** 4 servings (serving size: 1 cake).

Per serving: CALORIES 232 (33% from fat); FAT 8.5g (saturated fat 1.6g); PROTEIN 9.7g; CARBOHYDRATES 30.9g; FIBER 5.6g; CHOLESTEROL 90mg; IRON 2.7mg; SODIUM 597mg; CALCIUM 58mg

Red and Green Tomato Salad

prep: 7 minutes • **other:** 2 minutes   *POINTS* value: 1

Combine 1 chopped medium ripe tomato; 1 chopped medium green tomato; ½ peeled, seeded, and chopped avocado; 2 chopped medium pepperoncini peppers; 1 teaspoon pepperoncini liquid; 1 teaspoon extra-virgin olive oil; ¼ teaspoon salt; and ¼ teaspoon freshly ground black pepper in a medium bowl. Toss gently to coat. Let stand 2 minutes to absorb flavors. **Yield:** 4 servings (serving size: ½ cup).

Per serving: CALORIES 57 (65% from fat); FAT 4.1g (saturated fat 0.5g); PROTEIN 1.4g; CARBOHYDRATES 5.2g; FIBER 1.5g; CHOLESTEROL 0mg; IRON 0.5mg; SODIUM 212mg; CALCIUM 10mg

Curried Couscous with Chickpeas

prep: 10 minutes • **cook:** 5 minutes • **other:** 5 minutes   *POINTS* value: 6

The one-step simplicity of this meatless meal highlights the distinctive and powerful taste combination of earthy curry and sweet golden raisins. This recipe is delicious served hot or cold and stores well in the refrigerator for up to 3 days. For a creamy variation and an additional *POINTS* value of 1, stir ¼ cup fat-free Greek yogurt into the finished dish.

2	cups organic vegetable broth (such as Swanson Certified Organic)
½	cup golden raisins
1	teaspoon curry powder
½	teaspoon garlic salt
½	teaspoon olive oil
¼	teaspoon ground cumin
¼	teaspoon freshly ground black pepper
1	cup frozen petite green peas
1	(10-ounce) box plain couscous
¼	cup thinly sliced green onions
⅓	cup sliced almonds, toasted
1	(16-ounce) can chickpeas (garbanzo beans), rinsed and drained

1. Combine first 7 ingredients in a medium saucepan; bring to a boil over medium-high heat. Stir in peas and couscous; cover. Remove from heat; let stand 5 minutes. Add green onions, almonds, and chickpeas; fluff gently with a fork. **Yield:** 6 servings (serving size: 1 cup).

Per serving: CALORIES 307 (15% from fat); FAT 5.2g (saturated fat 0.5g); PROTEIN 10.6g; CARBOHYDRATES 57.7g; FIBER 5.7g; CHOLESTEROL 0mg; IRON 2.5mg; SODIUM 366mg; CALCIUM 54mg

---

Menu
POINTS value
per serving: 6

Curried Couscous with Chickpeas

Game Plan

1. While broth comes to a boil:
  • Rinse and drain chickpeas.

2. While couscous cooks:
  • Toast almonds.
  • Chop green onions.

3. Fluff couscous.

pictured on page 41

Grilled Vegetable Napoleons

prep: 11 minutes • **cook:** 6 minutes   *POINTS* value: 7

Menu
POINTS value
per serving: 8

Grilled Vegetable Napoleons

Spinach Salad with
Lemon-Parmesan Dressing

Game Plan

1. While grill heats:
- Slice polenta and vegetables.
- Prepare salad dressing.

2. While polenta and vegetables cook:
- Prepare vinaigrette for Napoleons.

3. Assemble Napoleons.

4. Toss salad.

Make sure your grill is nice and hot to create grill marks on the vegetables and polenta. To serve this dish family-style, arrange the polenta slices on a platter, and spoon the vegetables over the top of the polenta. Sprinkle the veggies with goat cheese, and drizzle with the basil vinaigrette.

- 1   (17-ounce) tube of polenta, cut into 12 slices
- 8   (¼-inch-thick) slices eggplant (about 8 ounces)
- 8   (¼-inch-thick) slices fennel bulb (about 7 ounces)
- 8   (¼-inch-thick) slices red onion (about 8 ounces)
- Cooking spray
- 1   tablespoon basil paste (such as Gourmet Garden Basil Herb Blend)
- 1   tablespoon red wine vinegar
- 1   tablespoon olive oil
- 1   large tomato, cut into 8 slices
- ½   cup (4 ounces) goat cheese, crumbled

1. Prepare grill.

2. Place polenta and next three ingredients on grill rack coated with cooking spray. Grill 3 minutes on each side or until vegetables are crisp-tender.

3. Combine basil paste, vinegar, and oil in a small bowl; stir well with a whisk.

4. To assemble each of 4 Napoleons, layer 1 polenta slice, 1 eggplant slice, 1 fennel slice, 1 onion slice, and 1 tomato slice. Drizzle each tomato slice with 1 teaspoon basil vinaigrette; repeat layers, ending with remaining polenta slice. Top evenly with crumbled goat cheese, and drizzle with remaining teaspoon of vinaigrette. **Yield:** 4 servings (serving size: 1 Napoleon).

Per serving: CALORIES 314 (35% from fat); FAT 12.3g (saturated fat 6.4g); PROTEIN 10.3g; CARBOHYDRATES 39.8g; FIBER 6g; CHOLESTEROL 22.4mg; IRON 1.2mg; SODIUM 750mg; CALCIUM 132mg

Spinach Salad with Lemon-Parmesan Dressing

prep: 3 minutes   *POINTS* value: 1

Combine 2 tablespoons grated fresh Parmigiano-Reggiano cheese; 1 tablespoon olive oil; 1 teaspoon grated lemon rind; 1 tablespoon fresh lemon juice; 1 teaspoon white wine vinegar; and 1 small shallot, peeled and sliced, in a large bowl. Stir well with a whisk. Add 1 (6-ounce) package fresh baby spinach; toss gently to coat. **Yield:** 4 servings (serving size: 1½ cups).

Per serving: CALORIES 65 (62% from fat); FAT 4.5g (saturated fat 1g); PROTEIN 2.6g; CARBOHYDRATES 5.2g; FIBER 2.1g; CHOLESTEROL 3mg; IRON 0.5mg; SODIUM 130mg; CALCIUM 83mg

Roasted Vegetable Pasta

prep: 3 minutes • **cook:** 15 minutes   *POINTS* value: 6

This fresh and colorful pasta will delight your senses of smell, sight, and taste. When boiling the water for the penne, start with hot tap water, and cover the pot with a lid. This is a surefire way to speed up your cook time.

1½	pounds thin asparagus spears
1	cup matchstick-cut carrots
1	small onion, halved and thinly sliced (about 1 cup)
1	pint grape tomatoes
1	garlic clove, pressed
1	teaspoon olive oil
½	teaspoon salt
¼	teaspoon freshly ground black pepper
8	ounces uncooked multigrain penne (such as Barilla Plus)
1	cup frozen petite green peas
1	cup whipping cream
⅔	cup (2.7 ounces) shaved fresh Parmesan cheese
¼	cup chopped fresh basil

1. Preheat oven to 450°.

2. Snap off tough ends of asparagus, and cut asparagus into 2-inch pieces. Combine asparagus and next 4 ingredients in a large roasting pan. Drizzle with olive oil, and sprinkle with salt and pepper; toss gently to coat. Bake at 450° for 10 minutes; stir vegetables. Bake an additional 5 minutes or until vegetables are tender and lightly browned.

3. While vegetables roast, cook pasta according to package directions, omitting salt and fat. Drain well, reserving ⅓ cup pasta water. Keep pasta and reserved water warm.

4. Combine roasted vegetables, pasta, reserved ⅓ cup pasta water, peas, and whipping cream; toss gently to coat. Sprinkle with cheese and basil. Serve immediately.

Yield: 8 servings (serving size: 1¼ cups).

Per serving: CALORIES 293 (46% from fat); FAT 14.9g (saturated fat 8.5g); PROTEIN 12g; CARBOHYDRATES 30.5g; FIBER 5.7g; CHOLESTEROL 49mg; IRON 1.7mg; SODIUM 335mg; CALCIUM 167mg

Menu
POINTS value
per serving: 8

Roasted Vegetable Pasta

½ cup blood orange sorbet
POINTS value: 2

Game Plan

1. While oven preheats:
  • Prepare vegetables.

2. While vegetables cook:
  • Cook pasta.
  • Shave Parmesan cheese.
  • Chop basil.

3. Combine vegetables and pasta.

4. Scoop sorbet into serving bowls.

Menu
POINTS value
per serving: 7

Parmesan-Breaded Portobellos

**1 cup steamed pretrimmed
green beans**
POINTS value: 0

Game Plan

1. While water for pasta comes to a boil:
- Mince basil, and shred cheese.
- Prepare panko mixture.

2. While pasta cooks:
- Dredge mushrooms in panko mixture.

3. While mushrooms cook:
- Warm pasta sauce.
- Steam green beans in microwave.
- Toss pasta.

Parmesan-Breaded Portobellos

prep: 4 minutes • **cook:** 16 minutes   *POINTS* value: 7

Parmesan cheese and crunchy panko, also called Japanese bread-crumbs, form a delicate crust on these hearty portobellos. When breading the mushrooms, use one hand for the dry mixture and the other hand for the wet so you don't lose any panko crumbs or cheese.

  2 ounces uncooked whole wheat spaghetti
  ¼ cup panko (Japanese breadcrumbs)
  3 tablespoons shredded fresh Parmesan cheese
  2 tablespoons minced fresh basil
  ¼ teaspoon salt
  1 large egg
  1 large egg white
  4 (4-inch) portobello caps
1½ teaspoons olive oil
  1 cup low-sodium tomato-basil pasta sauce (such as Amy's Organic), warmed

1. Cook pasta according to package directions, omitting salt and fat; drain well.
2. While pasta cooks, combine panko, cheese, basil, and salt in a shallow dish; set aside.
3. Stir egg and egg white together with a whisk in a shallow dish. Dip each mushroom cap in egg mixture; dredge in panko mixture. Discard remaining egg mixture and panko mixture.
4. Heat oil in a large nonstick skillet over medium heat. Add mushroom caps to pan; cook 4 minutes or until lightly browned. Turn mushrooms, and cook 3 additional minutes.
5. Combine warm pasta sauce and pasta in a medium bowl; toss gently to coat. Place mushrooms over pasta, and serve immediately. **Yield:** 2 servings (serving size: 2 mushrooms and ½ cup pasta).

Per serving: CALORIES 350 (34% from fat); FAT 13.2g (saturated fat 3g); PROTEIN 17.9g; CARBOHYDRATES 44.3g; FIBER 8.1g; CHOLESTEROL 60mg; IRON 2mg; SODIUM 832mg; CALCIUM 185mg

Spinach-Artichoke Pizza

prep: 4 minutes • **cook:** 10 minutes

POINTS value: 3

Call your family to the table while this juicy veggie pizza is under the broiler so they will be ready to enjoy it right away. Baking the pizza crust in the oven while it preheats is the key to a crispy exterior.

1   (10-ounce) whole wheat Italian cheese-flavored thin pizza crust (such as Boboli)

Olive oil–flavored cooking spray

½   cup marinara sauce

⅔   cup (2½ ounces) shredded part-skim mozzarella cheese, divided

½   (5-ounce) package baby spinach (about 2 cups)

2   plum tomatoes, sliced (about 1 cup)

1   garlic clove, minced

½   cup canned artichokes hearts, drained and chopped

⅛   teaspoon crushed red pepper

1. Preheat oven to 450°.

2. While oven is preheating, place pizza crust directly on oven rack; bake 7 minutes or until crust is golden. Remove crust from oven, and place on a baking sheet.

3. Preheat broiler.

4. Coat pizza crust with cooking spray. Spread marinara sauce on crust, and sprinkle with ⅓ cup mozzarella cheese. Top with spinach, tomato, garlic, artichoke, and remaining ⅓ cup cheese.

5. Broil pizza 3 minutes or until cheese melts. Sprinkle with red pepper, and serve immediately. **Yield:** 6 servings (serving size: 1 slice).

Per serving: CALORIES 189 (26% from fat); FAT 5.4g (saturated fat 2.9g); PROTEIN 9.4g; CARBOHYDRATES 5.5g; FIBER 4.8g; CHOLESTEROL 6.8mg; IRON 1.5mg; SODIUM 442mg; CALCIUM 149mg

Menu
POINTS value
per serving: 3

Spinach-Artichoke Pizza

1 cup garden salad with fat-free balsamic vinaigrette
POINTS value: 0

Game Plan

1. While oven preheats:
- Bake crust.
- Prepare vegetables, and measure ingredients.

2. While pizza cooks:
- Prepare salad.

pictured on page 40

Pasta with Butternut Squash, Fried Rosemary, and Parmesan

Menu
POINTS value
per serving: 8

Pasta with Butternut Squash, Fried Rosemary, and Parmesan

Mixed Greens with Lemon and Olive Oil

Game Plan

1. While water for pasta comes to a boil:
- Prepare salad.
- Prepare sauce.

2. While pasta cooks and sauce simmers:
- Prepare rosemary-infused oil; add to sauce.

3. Toss pasta.

prep: 6 minutes • **cook:** 14 minutes   *POINTS* value: 7

Store the remaining rosemary-infused oil in an airtight container in the refrigerator for up to 2 weeks. Serve it over fresh vegetables.

  8 ounces whole wheat extra-wide egg noodles (such as Ronzoni)
  1 (12-ounce) package frozen pureed butternut squash (such as McKenzie's)
  1 tablespoon olive oil
  ½ cup diced onion
  2 garlic cloves, minced
  ½ cup organic vegetable broth
  1 tablespoon grated orange rind
  ⅓ cup fresh orange juice
  ⅛ teaspoon salt
  ¼ teaspoon freshly ground black pepper
  ⅓ cup olive oil
  3 (6-inch) rosemary sprigs
  ¼ cup freshly grated Parmigiano-Reggiano cheese

1. Cook pasta according to package directions, omitting salt and fat. Drain and keep warm.
2. While pasta cooks, microwave squash according to package directions. Heat 1 tablespoon oil in a large nonstick skillet over medium-high heat. Add onion and garlic to pan; sauté 2 minutes or until brown. Stir in squash, broth, rind, juice, salt, and pepper. Bring to a simmer; cook 4 minutes, stirring frequently.
3. While butternut sauce simmers and pasta cooks, heat ⅓ cup olive oil in a medium skillet over medium-high heat. Add rosemary sprigs to pan; cook 1 minute or until sizzling stops, turning once. Remove rosemary leaves. Drain on paper towels. Add 1 tablespoon rosemary-infused oil to sauce. Reserve remaining oil for another use.
4. Combine warm pasta and butternut sauce; toss gently to coat. Divide pasta among 4 bowls; sprinkle evenly with rosemary leaves and cheese. Serve immediately. **Yield:** 4 servings (serving size: 1 cup pasta and 1 tablespoon cheese).

Per serving: CALORIES 341 (31% from fat); FAT 11.8g (saturated fat 2.3g); PROTEIN 10.3g; CARBOHYDRATES 54.8g; FIBER 7.6g; CHOLESTEROL 4.4mg; IRON 2.6mg; SODIUM 430mg; CALCIUM 87mg

Mixed Greens with Lemon and Olive Oil

prep: 3 minutes   *POINTS* value: 1

Combine 1 (5-ounce) package mixed salad greens, 1 tablespoon extra-virgin olive oil, 1 tablespoon fresh lemon juice, and ⅛ teaspoon salt in a large bowl; toss gently to coat. Serve immediately. **Yield:** 4 servings (serving size: 1½ cups).

Per serving: CALORIES 36 (90% from fat); FAT 3.6g (saturated fat 0.5g); PROTEIN 0.6g; CARBOHYDRATES 1.2g; FIBER 0.8g; CHOLESTEROL 0mg; IRON 0.5mg; SODIUM 82mg; CALCIUM 20mg

Spring Vegetable Fried Rice

prep: 11 minutes • **cook:** 9 minutes   *POINTS* value: 7

Using precooked rice, frozen peas, and matchstick-cut carrots speeds up the preparation of this simple Chinese standby. Gently squeeze the unopened packages of rice to break up any lumps before adding the rice to the pan. If you have leftover rice on hand, use it in this recipe instead of the precooked variety.

1½   cups (1-inch) sliced asparagus (about 6 ounces)
½   cup matchstick-cut carrots
⅓   cup vegetable broth
3   tablespoons low-sodium soy sauce
1   teaspoon grated peeled fresh ginger
1   teaspoon dark sesame oil
¼   teaspoon salt
2   teaspoons canola oil, divided
Cooking spray
4   large eggs, lightly beaten
2   (8.8-ounce) packages precooked long-grain rice (such as Uncle Ben's Ready Rice)
½   cup frozen petite green peas, thawed
¼   cup thinly sliced green onions

1. Steam asparagus and carrots in a medium saucepan, covered, 2 minutes or until crisp-tender. Rinse with cold water; drain.
2. While vegetables steam, combine broth and next 4 ingredients in a medium bowl; stir with a whisk.
3. Heat 1 teaspoon canola oil in a large nonstick skillet coated with cooking spray over medium-high heat. Add egg to pan; cook, stirring constantly, 1 minute or until scrambled. Remove egg from pan.
4. Heat remaining 1 teaspoon canola oil in pan over medium-high heat. Add rice to pan; cook, stirring occasionally, 3 minutes or until thoroughly heated. Add steamed vegetables, broth mixture, scrambled egg, peas, and green onions; cook, stirring occasionally, 1 minute or until thoroughly heated. **Yield:** 4 servings (serving size: 1¼ cups).

Per serving: CALORIES 313 (31% from fat); FAT 10.9g (saturated fat 1.9g); PROTEIN 12.5g; CARBOHYDRATES 41.7g; FIBER 2.6g; CHOLESTEROL 212mg; IRON 3.2mg; SODIUM 776mg; CALCIUM 100mg

Menu
POINTS value
per serving: 8

Spring Vegetable Fried Rice

1 orange
POINTS value: 1

Game Plan

1. Chop and slice vegetables.

2. While vegetables steam:
 • Measure and prepare ingredients for broth mixture.

3. Scramble eggs.

4. Prepare rice mixture.

5. Slice oranges into wedges.

Menu
POINTS value
per serving: 8

**Tofu with Almonds and
Sugar Snap Peas**

Five-Spice Brown Rice

Game Plan

1. While water for rice comes to
a boil:
- Remove moisture from tofu.
- Toast almonds.
- Chop cilantro and green
onions; mince garlic.

2. While rice cooks:
- Prepare tofu mixture.

Tofu with Almonds and Sugar Snap Peas

prep: 9 minutes • **cook:** 9 minutes

POINTS value: 5

**In this easy Asian-inspired entrée, a sweet and savory soy sauce
mixture enlivens stir-fried tofu, while cilantro and green onions
offer a burst of fresh flavor.**

1   (14-ounce) package extra-firm tofu, drained
2   teaspoons dark sesame oil
1   (8-ounce) package fresh sugar snap peas
⅓   cup slivered almonds, toasted
2   garlic cloves, minced
3   tablespoons brown sugar
1   tablespoon low-sodium soy sauce
3   tablespoons chopped fresh cilantro
2   green onions, chopped

1. Place tofu on several layers of heavy-duty paper towels. Cover tofu with additional paper towels; gently press out moisture. Cut tofu in half crosswise. Cut each
half into ½-inch-thick slices.
2. Heat oil in a large nonstick skillet over medium-high heat. Add tofu to pan;
cook 3 minutes on each side or until browned. Add snap peas, almonds, and
garlic; sauté 1 minute. Add brown sugar and soy sauce; cook, stirring constantly,
1 minute or until sugar melts. Sprinkle with cilantro and green onions. Serve
immediately. **Yield:** 4 servings (serving size: ¾ cup).

Per serving: CALORIES 234 (46% from fat); FAT 12g (saturated fat 0.7g); PROTEIN 12.6g; CARBOHYDRATES 20.8g; FIBER 4.1g; CHOLESTEROL 0mg; IRON 3.4mg;
SODIUM 147mg; CALCIUM 272mg

Five-Spice Brown Rice

prep: 3 minutes • **cook:** 9 minutes • **other:** 5 minutes

POINTS value: 3

Bring 1¾ cups water to a boil. Add ½ teaspoon dark sesame oil, 1 tablespoon
low-sodium soy sauce, and 2 teaspoons five-spice powder to boiling water. Stir
in 2 cups instant brown rice. Cover, reduce heat to low, and simmer 5 minutes.
Remove from heat; let stand 5 minutes. Fluff rice with a fork. Serve immediately.
Yield: 4 servings (serving size: ½ cup).

Per serving: CALORIES 161 (13% from fat); FAT 2.3g (saturated fat 0.1g); PROTEIN 3.3g; CARBOHYDRATES 35.3g; FIBER 2g; CHOLESTEROL 0mg; IRON 1.1mg;
SODIUM 143mg; CALCIUM 12mg

Meats

pictured on page 45

Beef and Pepperoni Pizza

prep: 2 minutes • **cook:** 13 minutes   *POINTS* value: 7

We've reduced the fat, calories, and sodium in a pizzeria-style meat pizza by 50% without sacrificing the delicious and satisfying taste.

Menu
POINTS value
per serving: 8

Beef and Pepperoni Pizza

Classic Vinaigrette Salad

Game Plan

1. Prepare and measure ingredients for pizza.

2. While pizza bakes:
- Mince garlic.
- Prepare dressing.
- Slice cucumber and radishes.

3. Toss salad.

 1 (10-ounce) Italian thin whole wheat pizza crust (such as Boboli)
 ½ pound extra lean ground beef
 1 (8-ounce) package sliced fresh mushrooms
    Olive oil–flavored cooking spray
 ¾ cup marinara sauce (such as Newman's Own)
 ¼ cup turkey pepperoni (about 15 slices)
 ⅔ cup shredded part-skim mozzarella cheese
 ¼ teaspoon crushed red pepper

1. Preheat oven to 450°.
2. Place pizza crust on rack in oven while preheating; heat 5 minutes.
3. While crust heats, sauté beef and mushrooms in a large nonstick skillet coated with cooking spray over medium-high heat 5 minutes or until beef is browned; drain.
4. Remove crust from oven; place on an ungreased baking sheet. Coat crust with cooking spray; spread marinara sauce over crust, leaving a 1-inch border. Top with beef mixture, pepperoni, and cheese. Sprinkle evenly with red pepper.
5. Bake at 450° for 7 to 10 minutes or until crust is golden and cheese is melted. Cut into 8 wedges. Serve immediately. **Yield:** 4 servings (serving size: 2 slices).

Per serving: CALORIES 367 (28% from fat); FAT 11.5g (saturated fat 5.3g); PROTEIN 29.1g; CARBOHYDRATES 7.4g; FIBER 6.8g; CHOLESTEROL 49mg; IRON 2.8mg; SODIUM 810mg; CALCIUM 216mg

Classic Vinaigrette Salad

prep: 7 minutes   *POINTS* value: 1

Combine ¼ cup red wine vinegar, 1 tablespoon Dijon mustard, 2 teaspoons olive oil, 1 minced garlic clove, 1 teaspoon sugar, ¼ teaspoon salt, and ¼ teaspoon black pepper in a small bowl, stirring with a whisk. Combine 1 (6.5-ounce) package sweet butter lettuce blend, 2 cups thinly sliced cucumber, and 4 sliced radishes in a large bowl. Pour dressing over lettuce mixture; toss well. **Yield:** 4 servings (serving size: 2 cups).

Per serving: CALORIES 47 (44% from fat); FAT 2.3g (saturated fat 0.3g); PROTEIN 1.4g; CARBOHYDRATES 5.7g; FIBER 1.5g; CHOLESTEROL 0mg; IRON 0.4mg; SODIUM 250mg; CALCIUM 21mg

Garlic-Thyme Flank Steak

prep: 5 minutes • **cook:** 10 minutes • **other:** 5 minutes   *POINTS* value: 4

An easy rub featuring garlic and thyme gives the flank steak robust flavor. Scoring the steak diagonally in diamond-shaped patterns allows the seasonings to quickly penetrate the meat, eliminating the need for marinating.

    1   tablespoon chopped fresh thyme
    3   garlic cloves, pressed
    ½   teaspoon salt
    ½   teaspoon freshly ground black pepper
    2   teaspoons olive oil
    1   pound flank steak, trimmed
    Cooking spray

1. Prepare grill.
2. Combine first 5 ingredients in a small bowl.
3. Score both sides of steak diagonally in diamond-shaped patterns. Rub thyme mixture evenly over both sides of steak.
4. Place steak on grill rack coated with cooking spray; grill 5 minutes on each side or until desired degree of doneness. Remove from grill, and let stand 5 minutes. Cut steak diagonally across grain into thin slices. Yield: 4 servings (serving size: 3 ounces steak).

Per serving: CALORIES 185 (42% from fat); FAT 8.6g (saturated fat 2.7g); PROTEIN 24.7g; CARBOHYDRATES 1.1g; FIBER 0.2g; CHOLESTEROL 37mg; IRON 2mg; SODIUM 354mg; CALCIUM 35mg

Blue Cheese Mashed Potatoes

prep: 2 minutes • **cook:** 2 minutes   *POINTS* value: 3

Place 2 cups refrigerated mashed potatoes (such as Simply Potatoes) in a large microwave-safe bowl. Cover with plastic wrap; microwave at HIGH 2 minutes or until thoroughly heated. Stir in ½ cup crumbled blue cheese and ⅛ teaspoon freshly ground black pepper. Yield: 4 servings (serving size: ½ cup).

Per serving: CALORIES 125 (37% from fat); FAT 5.1g (saturated fat 2.5g); PROTEIN 4.5g; CARBOHYDRATES 15.5g; FIBER 1.5g; CHOLESTEROL 13mg; IRON 0.3mg; SODIUM 467mg; CALCIUM 90mg

---

Menu
POINTS value
per serving: 7

Garlic-Thyme Flank Steak

Blue Cheese Mashed Potatoes

1 cup mixed baby greens with fat-free balsamic vinaigrette
POINTS value: 0

Game Plan

1. While grill heats:
  • Prepare thyme mixture.
  • Score diamond-shaped patterns on steak; rub with thyme mixture.

2. Grill steak.

3. While steak stands:
  • Prepare potatoes.
  • Toss greens with vinaigrette.

4. Slice steak.

Menu
POINTS value
per serving: 7

Orange-Chipotle Flank Steak

Orange Mashed Sweet Potatoes

1 cup steamed
pretrimmed green beans
POINTS value: 0

Game Plan

1. While grill heats:
  • Prepare orange mixture.

2. While steak cooks:
  • Microwave potatoes.

3. While steak stands:
  • Steam green beans in microwave.
  • Prepare and mash potatoes.

4. Slice steak.

Orange-Chipotle Flank Steak

prep: 5 minutes • **cook:** 10 minutes • **other:** 5 minutes   *POINTS* value: 5

The smokiness of the chipotle chile sauce complements the concentrated citrus flavor in this entrée. You'll only need the sauce from the can of chiles. Freeze the peppers to use later.

  2 tablespoons thawed orange juice concentrate
  1 tablespoon adobo sauce from canned chipotle chiles
  2 teaspoons low-sodium soy sauce
  2 teaspoons olive oil
  1 garlic clove, pressed
  1 pound flank steak
Cooking spray

1. Prepare grill.
2. Combine first 5 ingredients in a small bowl.
3. Baste steak with orange mixture. Place steak on grill rack coated with cooking spray; grill 5 minutes on each side or until desired degree of doneness, basting occasionally with orange mixture. Remove from grill, and let stand 5 minutes. Cut steak diagonally across grain into thin slices. **Yield:** 4 servings (serving size: 3 ounces steak).

Per serving: CALORIES 199 (39% from fat); FAT 8.6g (saturated fat 2.7g); PROTEIN 24.9g; CARBOHYDRATES 4.3g; FIBER 0.4g; CHOLESTEROL 37mg; IRON 2mg; SODIUM 192mg; CALCIUM 32mg

Orange Mashed Sweet Potatoes

prep: 4 minutes • **cook:** 6 minutes   *POINTS* value: 2

Place 3½ cups frozen cut sweet potatoes (such as Ore Ida) in a medium microwave-safe bowl. Microwave at HIGH 6 minutes or until potatoes are tender, stirring after 3 minutes. Add 2 tablespoons yogurt-based spread (such as Brummel & Brown), 1 tablespoon brown sugar, 1 tablespoon fat-free milk, 1 teaspoon grated orange rind, and ⅛ teaspoon salt to potatoes. Mash with a potato masher until desired consistency. Serve immediately. **Yield:** 4 servings (serving size: ½ cup).

Per serving: CALORIES 111 (20% from fat); FAT 2.5g (saturated fat 0.5g); PROTEIN 1g; CARBOHYDRATES 20g; FIBER 2.7g; CHOLESTEROL 0mg; IRON 0.4mg; SODIUM 147mg; CALCIUM 25mg

Grilled Flank Steak Fajitas

prep: 5 minutes • **cook:** 10 minutes • **other:** 5 minutes   *POINTS* value: 6

Grilling the flank steak and the vegetables at the same time makes these sizzling fajitas fast to prepare. Thinly slice the flank steak against the grain to ensure a tender bite.

    1   pound flank steak
    ⅓   cup fresh lime juice
    2   tablespoons fajita seasoning
    1   medium red bell pepper, halved and seeded
    1   medium green bell pepper, halved and seeded
        Cooking spray
    6   (8-inch) 96% fat-free flour tortillas, warmed
    1   cup preshredded lettuce
    1   cup chopped tomato
    ¾   cup (3-ounces) reduced-fat shredded sharp Cheddar cheese
    1   cup refrigerated fresh salsa
    ¼   cup reduced-fat sour cream
        Chopped fresh cilantro

1. Prepare grill.
2. Combine steak, lime juice, and fajita seasoning in a shallow baking dish.
3. Place steak and peppers on a grill rack coated with cooking spray; grill 5 minutes on each side or until steak is desired degree of doneness and peppers are tender. Remove from grill, and let stand 5 minutes.
4. Cut peppers into thin strips. Cut steak diagonally across the grain into thin slices. Divide steak and peppers evenly among tortillas and top evenly with lettuce, tomatoes, cheese, salsa, sour cream, and cilantro. **Yield:** 6 servings (serving size: 1 fajita).

Per serving: CALORIES 318 (25% from fat); FAT 8.8g (saturated fat 3.6g); PROTEIN 24.5g; CARBOHYDRATES 32.9g; FIBER 4.1g; CHOLESTEROL 35mg; IRON 3.4mg; SODIUM 695mg; CALCIUM 230mg

Avocado and Black Bean Salsa Salad

prep: 6 minutes   *POINTS* value: 1

Rinse and drain 1 (15-ounce) can black beans. Combine beans, 1 cup refrigerated fresh salsa, 1 peeled and diced avocado, ¼ cup chopped fresh cilantro, 1 tablespoon fresh lime juice, and ½ teaspoon cumin in a medium bowl. Toss well. **Yield:** 6 servings (serving size: ½ cup).

Per serving: CALORIES 83 (41% from fat); FAT 3.8g (saturated fat 0.4g); PROTEIN 2.8g; CARBOHYDRATES 10.7g; FIBER 3.2g; CHOLESTEROL 0mg; IRON 1mg; SODIUM 220mg; CALCIUM 17mg

---

Menu
POINTS value
per serving: 7

Grilled Flank Steak Fajitas

Avocado and Black Bean Salsa Salad

Game Plan

1. While grill heats:
  • Prepare lime juice mixture for steak.
  • Halve and seed peppers.
  • Rinse and drain beans.
  • Peel and dice avocado.
  • Chop cilantro.

2. Grill steak and peppers.

3. While steak stands:
  • Prepare salad.
  • Chop tomato.
  • Slice peppers.

4. Slice steak, and assemble fajitas.

Game Plan

1. Slice pepper and onion; mince ginger.

2. While vegetables cook:
 • Slice flank steak.

3. While steak cooks:
 • Chop mango and cilantro.
 • Warm tortillas.

4. Assemble tacos.

Mango Beef Tacos

prep: 5 minutes • **cook:** 15 minutes   *POINTS* value: 7

You'll enjoy the tantalizing aroma as you prepare these flank steak tacos. Fresh mango and ginger give this dish a Caribbean flair.

  2 teaspoons olive oil
  2 cups julienne-cut red bell pepper, (about 1 medium)
  1 cup thinly sliced onion
  2 teaspoons minced fresh ginger
 12 ounces flank steak, trimmed
  4 teaspoons low-sodium soy sauce
  1 teaspoon chili powder
  8 (6-inch) whole wheat tortillas (such as Mission Fajita Carb Balance)
  1 cup chopped mango (about 1)
  ½ cup refrigerated fresh salsa
  ¼ cup chopped fresh cilantro
Reduced-fat sour cream, optional

1. Heat oil in a large nonstick skillet over medium-high heat. Add bell pepper, onion, and ginger; cook 6 minutes or until tender, stirring often.
2. While vegetable mixture cooks, cut steak diagonally across grain into thin slices. Add steak to pan; cook 5 minutes or until browned. Add soy sauce and chili powder; cook 1 minute.
3. Warm tortillas according to package directions. Divide steak and pepper mixture evenly among tortillas and top evenly with mango, salsa, and cilantro. Serve with sour cream, if desired. **Yield:** 4 servings (serving size: 2 tacos).

Per serving: CALORIES 364 (28% from fat); FAT 11.2g (saturated fat 2.2g); PROTEIN 25.6g; CARBOHYDRATES 38.1g; FIBER 18.1g; CHOLESTEROL 28mg; IRON 2.3mg; SODIUM 827mg; CALCIUM 116mg

pictured on page 44

Ginger-Teriyaki Strip Steaks

prep: 5 minutes • **cook:** 10 minutes • **other:** 5 minutes **POINTS** value: 4

Strip steaks are very tender and full of flavor, which makes them a great choice to broil or grill. One steak will generally weigh close to 8 ounces when purchased raw because it's a long, thick cut of meat. For portion control and to keep this recipe budget-friendly, we've called for 2 (8-ounce) steaks, cut in half.

     2   tablespoons low-sodium soy sauce
     2   tablespoons low-sodium teriyaki sauce
     1   tablespoon honey
     1   garlic clove, minced
    1½   teaspoons grated peeled fresh ginger
     ⅛   teaspoon crushed red pepper
     2   (8-ounce) beef strip steaks, cut in half
    Cooking spray

1. Preheat broiler.
2. Combine first 6 ingredients in a small bowl, stirring with a whisk.
3. Place steaks on a broiler pan coated with cooking spray. Baste steaks evenly with 1 tablespoon soy sauce mixture.
4. Broil 5 minutes on each side or until desired degree of doneness, basting with remaining soy sauce mixture. Remove from oven. Let stand 5 minutes. **Yield:** 4 servings (serving size: 3 ounces steak).

Per serving: CALORIES 181 (25% from fat); FAT 5.1g (saturated fat 2g); PROTEIN 25.4g; CARBOHYDRATES 7g; FIBER 0.1g; CHOLESTEROL 67mg; IRON 2.2mg; SODIUM 494mg; CALCIUM 9mg

Cucumber Salad

prep: 10 minutes **POINTS** value: 1

Combine ⅓ cup rice vinegar, 2 teaspoons olive oil, and 2 tablespoons sugar in a small bowl, stirring with a whisk. Set aside. Combine 2 cups thinly sliced English cucumber, 1 small red bell pepper (seeded and thinly sliced), ¾ cup matchstick-cut carrots, 2 chopped green onions, and ¼ cup chopped fresh mint in a large bowl. Pour vinegar mixture over cucumber mixture; toss gently to coat. **Yield:** 4 servings (serving size: 1 cup).

Per serving: CALORIES 64 (35% from fat); FAT 2.5g (saturated fat 0.4g); PROTEIN 0.9g; CARBOHYDRATES 10.7g; FIBER 1.4g; CHOLESTEROL 0mg; IRON 0.5mg; SODIUM 4mg; CALCIUM 21mg

Menu
POINTS value
per serving: 5

Ginger-Teriyaki Strip Steaks

Cucumber Salad

Game Plan

1. While broiler preheats:
 • Prepare soy sauce mixture for steaks.
 • Prepare dressing for salad.

2. While steaks cook:
 • Slice cucumber and pepper; chop green onions and mint.

3. While steaks stand:
 • Toss salad.

pictured on page 42

Beef Fillets with Cranberry-Wine Sauce

prep: 7 minutes • **cook:** 11 minutes   *POINTS* value: 5

Dry red wine balances the tartness of cranberries in the sweet and savory sauce for these melt-in-your-mouth tenderloins. For a non-alcoholic alternative, substitute pomegranate juice for the wine.

4   (4-ounce) beef tenderloin steaks (½ to ¾ inch thick), trimmed
¼   teaspoon salt
⅛   teaspoon freshly ground black pepper
2   teaspoons olive oil
2   shallots, chopped
1   garlic clove, minced
¼   cup dry red wine
¼   cup fat-free, less-sodium beef broth
1   cup fresh cranberries
1   tablespoon light brown sugar
1   teaspoon finely chopped fresh rosemary
Rosemary leaves (optional)

1. Sprinkle steaks with salt and pepper.
2. Heat oil in a large nonstick skillet over medium-high heat; add steaks to pan. Cook 2 to 3 minutes on each side or until desired degree of doneness. Remove from heat; keep warm.
3. Reduce heat to medium. Add shallots and garlic to pan; sauté 1 to 2 minutes or until softened. Increase heat to medium-high; add wine, broth, and cranberries to pan. Cook 5 minutes, stirring often, until cranberries pop and liquid thickens. Stir in brown sugar and rosemary. Serve sauce over steaks. Garnish with rosemary leaves, if desired. **Yield:** 4 servings (serving size: 3 ounces steak and 2 tablespoons sauce).

Per serving: CALORIES 205 (38% from fat); FAT 8.7g (saturated fat 2.7g); PROTEIN 22.3g; CARBOHYDRATES 7.3g; FIBER 1.2g; CHOLESTEROL 59mg; IRON 1.6mg; SODIUM 221mg; CALCIUM 24mg

Sweet Potatoes with Orange Butter

prep: 3 minutes • **cook:** 8 minutes • **other:** 5 minutes   *POINTS* value: 3

Microwave 4 (6-ounce) sweet potatoes at HIGH 8 to 9 minutes or until tender, rearranging after 5 minutes. Wrap potatoes in towel. Let stand 5 minutes. While sweet potatoes cook, combine 2 tablespoons yogurt-based spread (such as Brummel & Brown), 1 teaspoon grated orange rind, ¼ teaspoon salt, and ⅛ teaspoon freshly ground black pepper in a small bowl. Cut potatoes in half within ½ inch of bottom, and push open. Fluff sweet potatoes with a fork, and top with orange butter. **Yield:** 4 servings (serving size: 1 potato and 1½ teaspoons orange butter).

Per serving: CALORIES 169 (14% from fat); FAT 2.6g (saturated fat 0.5g); PROTEIN 2.7g; CARBOHYDRATES 34.4g; FIBER 5.2g; CHOLESTEROL 0mg; IRON 1.1mg; SODIUM 284mg; CALCIUM 52mg

---

Menu
POINTS value
per serving: 8

Beef Fillets with Cranberry-Wine Sauce

Sweet Potatoes with Orange Butter

Game Plan

1. Chop shallots and rosemary; mince garlic.

2. While potatoes cook:
 • Cook steaks.
 • Prepare orange butter for potatoes.

3. While potatoes stand:
 • Cook sauce for steaks.

4. Assemble potatoes.

Beef Fillets with Sherry-Shiitake Sauce

prep: 5 minutes • **cook:** 12 minutes   *POINTS* value: 5

There's no need to go to an expensive steak house when you can make a restaurant-quality dinner at home for less than half the price. If you'd like, substitute regular button mushrooms for the shiitakes.

4	(4-ounce) beef tenderloin steaks (½ to ¾ inch thick), trimmed
½	teaspoon salt
¼	teaspoon black pepper
1	teaspoon olive oil, divided
	Cooking spray
¼	cup chopped shallots
4½	cups shiitake mushrooms (about 7 ounces), sliced
½	teaspoon minced garlic
⅓	cup dry sherry
¾	cup less-sodium beef stock (such as Swanson's)
½	teaspoon Dijon mustard

1. Sprinkle both sides of steaks with salt and pepper.

2. Heat ½ teaspoon oil in a large nonstick skillet coated with cooking spray over medium-high heat. Add steaks to pan; cook 2 to 3 minutes on each side or until browned. Remove from pan; keep warm.

3. Heat remaining ½ teaspoon oil in pan; add shallots, mushrooms, and garlic to pan. Cook 3 minutes or until tender, stirring occasionally. Add sherry to pan; cook 1 minute or until liquid is almost evaporated. Stir in stock and mustard; bring to a boil. Return steaks to pan, and cook 3 minutes or until desired degree of doneness, turning once. **Yield:** 4 servings (serving size: 3 ounces steak and about ¼ cup sauce).

Per serving: CALORIES 208 (32% from fat); FAT 7.5g (saturated fat 2.6g); PROTEIN 24.1g; CARBOHYDRATES 5.2g; FIBER 0.7g; CHOLESTEROL 59mg; IRON 2.4mg; SODIUM 466mg; CALCIUM 20mg

Soft Polenta with Parmesan

prep: 2 minutes • **cook:** 5 minutes   *POINTS* value: 3

Bring 1 cup fat-free, less-sodium chicken broth; 1 cup fat-free milk; ⅛ teaspoon salt; and ¼ teaspoon black pepper to a boil in a medium saucepan. Stir with a whisk. Slowly add ½ cup yellow cornmeal to broth mixture, stirring with a whisk. Reduce heat to low. Cook, stirring constantly, 3 minutes or until thickened. Remove from heat; stir in ¼ cup (1 ounce) freshly grated Parmesan cheese, and serve immediately. **Yield:** 4 servings (serving size: ½ cup).

Per serving: CALORIES 130 (14% from fat); FAT 2g (saturated fat 1g); PROTEIN 7.4g; CARBOHYDRATES 19.6g; FIBER 1g; CHOLESTEROL 6mg; IRON 0.5mg; SODIUM 373mg; CALCIUM 176mg

---

Menu
POINTS value
per serving: 8

Beef Fillets with Sherry-Shiitake Sauce

Soft Polenta with Parmesan

Game Plan

1. Chop shallots, mince garlic, and slice mushrooms.

2. While steaks cook:
- Measure sherry, stock, and mustard for sauce.
- Measure broth, milk, and cornmeal for polenta.

3. While sauce cooks:
- Prepare polenta.

Menu
POINTS value
per serving: 8

Veal Parmigiana

Angel Hair Pasta with
Sun-Dried Tomatoes

Game Plan

1. While water for pasta comes to
a boil:
- Preheat broiler.
- Prepare seasoning for veal.
- Heat skillet.
- Dredge veal.

2. While pasta cooks:
- Cook veal.
- Chop sun-dried tomato halves
and parsley.
- Heat marinara sauce.

3. While veal broils:
- Toss pasta.

Veal Parmigiana

prep: 10 minutes • **cook:** 8 minutes   *POINTS* value: 7

**If you use veal chops instead of cutlets, place the chops between
2 sheets of plastic wrap; pound them with a meat mallet or small
heavy skillet to ¼-inch thickness.**

- ⅓ cup dry breadcrumbs
- ¼ cup grated Parmesan cheese, divided
- 1½ teaspoons dried Italian seasoning
- ½ teaspoon garlic powder
- ¼ teaspoon salt
- 4 (4-ounce) veal cutlets (about ¼ inch thick)
- 1 tablespoon olive oil
- Cooking spray
- 1 egg white, lightly beaten
- 2 cups marinara sauce (such as Amy's Organic Marinara Sauce)
- ½ cup (2 ounces) shredded part-skim mozzarella cheese

1. Preheat broiler.
2. Combine breadcrumbs, 2 tablespoons Parmesan cheese, Italian seasoning, and
garlic powder in a shallow dish.
3. Sprinkle salt over cutlets.
4. Heat oil in a large ovenproof skillet coated with cooking spray over medium-
high heat. Pour egg white into a shallow dish. Dip each cutlet in egg white; dredge
in breadcrumb mixture. Add veal to pan, and cook 2 minutes on each side or until
lightly browned and done. Remove from heat.
5. While cutlets cook, pour marinara sauce in a 2-cup glass measure. Microwave
at HIGH 1½ minutes or until thoroughly heated. Pour sauce over cutlets in pan.
Sprinkle with mozzarella cheese and remaining 2 tablespoons Parmesan cheese.
6. Broil 2 minutes or until cheese melts and is lightly browned. **Yield:** 4 servings
(serving size: 3 ounces veal and ½ cup sauce).

Per serving: CALORIES 311 (31% from fat); FAT 10.7g (saturated fat 3.6g); PROTEIN 33.8g; CARBOHYDRATES 18.6g; FIBER 2.4g; CHOLESTEROL 101mg;
IRON 2.9mg; SODIUM 885mg; CALCIUM 187mg

Angel Hair Pasta with Sun-Dried Tomatoes

prep: 4 minutes • **cook:** 14 minutes   *POINTS* value: 1

Cook 4 ounces multigrain pasta according to package directions, omitting salt and
fat; drain. Add 2 tablespoons chopped, drained oil-packed sun-dried tomato halves
and 2 tablespoons chopped fresh parsley to pasta; toss gently to coat. **Yield:** 4 servings (serving size: about ½ cup).

Per serving: CALORIES 107 (8% from fat); FAT 1g (saturated fat 0.1g); PROTEIN 4.4g; CARBOHYDRATES 22.2g; FIBER 3.9g; CHOLESTEROL 0mg; IRON 1.2mg;
SODIUM 12mg; CALCIUM 16mg

Moroccan Lamb and Couscous Bowl

prep: 3 minutes • **cook:** 10 minutes • **other:** 7 minutes   *POINTS* value: 6

Precubed butternut squash keeps the preparation time short for this meal. Look for it in the produce section of your supermarket. If you can't find the precubed variety, you can peel and cube an 8- to 10-ounce butternut squash.

    Cooking spray
  1 pound lean ground lamb
1½ cups (½-inch) precubed peeled butternut squash
  2 teaspoons ground cumin
 ¼ teaspoon ground cinnamon
  1 (14.5-ounce) can Mexican-style stewed tomatoes with jalapeño pepper and spices, undrained and chopped
  1 (14-ounce) can fat-free, less-sodium chicken broth
  1 cup couscous
 ¼ cup chopped fresh cilantro

1. Heat a large saucepan or Dutch oven over medium-high heat. Coat pan with cooking spray. Add lamb and squash to pan; cook 6 minutes or until lamb is browned, stirring frequently. Drain, and return to pan.
2. Add cumin and next 3 ingredients to pan. Bring to a boil; cook 4 minutes. Stir in couscous; cover, remove from heat, and let stand 7 minutes. Add cilantro, and fluff with a fork. **Yield:** 6 servings (serving size: about 1 cup).

Per serving: CALORIES 308 (31% from fat); FAT 10.5g (saturated fat 4.2g); PROTEIN 18.7g; CARBOHYDRATES 34.9g; FIBER 4g; CHOLESTEROL 50mg; IRON 2.1mg; SODIUM 457mg; CALCIUM 65mg

Wilted Sesame Spinach

prep: 1 minute • **cook:** 5 minutes   *POINTS* value: 0

Heat 1 teaspoon dark sesame oil in a large skillet coated with cooking spray over medium heat. Add 1 (5-ounce) package fresh baby spinach to pan; sauté 1 minute or until spinach wilts. Add additional (5-ounce) package fresh baby spinach to pan; sauté 1 minute or until spinach wilts. Sprinkle with 1 teaspoon toasted sesame seeds and ¼ teaspoon salt; toss well. **Yield:** 6 servings (serving size: about ⅓ cup).

Per serving: CALORIES 20 (54% from FAT); FAT 1.2g (saturated fat 0.2g); PROTEIN 1.4g; CARBOHYDRATES 1.8g; FIBER 1.1g; CHOLESTEROL 0mg; IRON 1.3mg; SODIUM 134mg; CALCIUM 47mg

Game Plan

1. Brown lamb mixture; drain.

2. While lamb mixture simmers with tomatoes and broth:
 • Toast sesame seeds.
 • Chop cilantro.

3. While lamb and couscous mixture stands:
 • Cook spinach.

Menu

POINTS value
per serving: 8

Greek Lamb Chops

Minted Pea Puree

Game Plan

1. While grill heats and lamb marinates:
   - Cook peas.
   - Chop mint.
   - Zest and juice lemon.

2. Grill lamb.

3. Puree pea mixture.

Greek Lamb Chops

prep: 3 minutes • **cook:** 10 minutes • **other:** 5 minutes   *POINTS* value: 6

We recommend serving these chops cooked medium-rare. If you prefer to cook them to a greater degree of doneness, be sure to remove the lamb from the grill at a slightly lower degree of doneness than you prefer. The temperature of the meat will rise about 5 to 10 degrees upon standing.

> 1 small garlic clove, pressed
> 2 teaspoons dried oregano
> 2 tablespoons fresh lemon juice
> 1 tablespoon olive oil
> 8 (4-ounce) lamb loin chops, trimmed
> Cooking spray
> ¼ cup (1 ounce) crumbled feta cheese

1. Prepare grill.
2. Combine first 4 ingredients in a large heavy-duty zip-top plastic bag. Add lamb chops to bag; seal. Marinate at room temperature 5 minutes.
3. Place lamb chops on a grill rack coated with cooking spray; grill 5 minutes on each side or until desired degree of doneness. Transfer lamb to a serving platter; sprinkle evenly with cheese. **Yield:** 4 servings (serving size: 2 lamb chops).

Per serving: CALORIES 260 (50% from fat); FAT 14.3g (saturated fat 4.9g); PROTEIN 29.7g; CARBOHYDRATES 1.7g; FIBER 0.4g; CHOLESTEROL 97mg; IRON 2.4mg; SODIUM 305mg; CALCIUM 67mg

Minted Pea Puree

prep: 4 minutes • **cook:** 5 minutes   *POINTS* value: 2

Combine 4 cups frozen peas, 1 cup water, and 1 garlic clove in a large saucepan; bring to a boil. Reduce heat, and simmer 3 minutes. Drain, reserving ¼ cup cooking liquid. Process pea mixture, reserved liquid, 1 teaspoon lemon rind, 1½ tablespoons fresh lemon juice, 2 tablespoons chopped mint, 1 teaspoon olive oil, 1 teaspoon butter, ½ teaspoon lemon pepper, and ⅛ teaspoon salt in a food processor 1 minute or until smooth. Serve immediately. **Yield:** 4 servings (serving size: about ⅔ cup).

Per serving: CALORIES 116 (20% from fat); FAT 2.6g (saturated fat 0.9g); PROTEIN 6.5g; CARBOHYDRATES 17.6g; FIBER 5.4g; CHOLESTEROL 3mg; IRON 2.2mg; SODIUM 270mg; CALCIUM 35mg

Spice-Rubbed Lamb Chops

prep: 6 minutes • **cook:** 8 minutes   *POINTS* value: 5

Delight your palate with these succulent lamb chops sprinkled with a fragrant Middle Eastern–inspired dry rub made of a few pantry herbs and spices. On warmer days when you're dining al fresco, grill these lamb chops instead of broiling them.

    1   teaspoon ground cumin
    1   teaspoon ground coriander
    ½   teaspoon salt
    ½   teaspoon freshly ground black pepper
    ½   teaspoon garlic powder
    ½   teaspoon paprika
    ¼   teaspoon sugar
    ¼   teaspoon ground red pepper
    8   (3-ounce) lamb loin chops, trimmed
    Cooking spray

1. Preheat broiler.

2. Combine first 8 ingredients in a small bowl; stir well to combine.

3. Rub spice mixture on both sides of lamb chops. Place lamb chops on a broiler pan coated with cooking spray; broil 4 to 5 minutes on each side or until desired degree of doneness. **Yield:** 4 servings (serving size: 2 chops).

Per serving: CALORIES 212 (40% from fat); FAT 9.4g (saturated fat 3.3g); PROTEIN 28.8g; CARBOHYDRATES 1.1g; FIBER 0.4g; CHOLESTEROL 90mg; IRON 2.2mg; SODIUM 372mg; CALCIUM 25mg

Cilantro-Almond Couscous

prep: 6 minutes • **cook:** 2 minutes • **other:** 5 minutes   *POINTS* value: 3

Combine ⅔ cup fat-free, less-sodium chicken broth and ¼ teaspoon salt in a medium saucepan. Bring to a boil; gradually stir in ⅔ cup couscous. Remove from heat; cover and let stand 5 minutes. Add ⅔ cup chopped fresh cilantro, ¼ cup toasted slivered almonds, ¼ cup chopped green onions, and 1½ teaspoons olive oil; fluff with a fork. **Yield:** 4 servings (serving size: ½ cup).

Per serving: CALORIES 168 (29% from fat); FAT 5.4g (saturated fat 0.6g); PROTEIN 5.8g; CARBOHYDRATES 24.4g; FIBER 2.5g; CHOLESTEROL 0mg; IRON 0.7mg; SODIUM 246mg; CALCIUM 30mg

---

Menu
POINTS value
per serving: 8

Spice-Rubbed Lamb Chops

Cilantro-Almond Couscous

Game Plan

1. While broiler preheats:
- Chop cilantro and green onions.
- Prepare spice mixture, and rub on lamb.

2. While lamb cooks:
- Bring broth to a boil.
- Let couscous stand.
- Toast almonds.

3. Prepare couscous.

Game Plan

1. While oven preheats:
- Chop basil and parsley.
- Season tomatoes.
- Season lamb chops.

2. While tomatoes bake:
- Cook broth mixture.
- Cook lamb chops.

3. Prepare potato mixture.

Lamb Chops with Skordalia

prep: 4 minutes • **cook:** 11 minutes   *POINTS* value: 6

A package of refrigerated mashed potatoes jump-starts this version of skordalia, a Greek sauce that's traditionally made with pureed potatoes.

1	lemon, halved and divided
8	(4-ounce) lamb loin chops, trimmed
2	teaspoons salt-free Greek seasoning
¼	teaspoon salt
¼	teaspoon black pepper
¼	cup fat-free, less-sodium chicken broth
6	garlic cloves, pressed
1	teaspoon olive oil
1	tablespoon water
½	cup fat-free milk
1¼	cups refrigerated mashed potatoes (such as Simply Potatoes)

1. Squeeze half of lemon over both sides of lamb chops. Sprinkle lamb evenly with Greek seasoning, salt, and pepper. Set aside.

2. Bring broth and garlic to a boil over medium-high heat. Reduce heat to low, and simmer 7 minutes or until broth almost evaporates.

3. While broth mixture cooks, heat oil in a large nonstick skillet over medium-high heat. Add lamb chops to pan; cook 3 minutes on each side or until desired degree of doneness. Remove from pan, and keep warm. Add water to pan, and cook 30 seconds, stirring to loosen browned bits from bottom of pan. Spoon pan juices over lamb chops.

4. Add milk to broth mixture, and bring to a boil over medium heat. Stir in potatoes until smooth. Cook 1 minute or until thoroughly heated. Spoon potato mixture evenly onto 4 serving plates. Place 2 lamb chops atop potatoes on each plate. Drizzle lamb evenly with accumulated juices. Cut remaining lemon half into 4 wedges, and serve with lamb. **Yield:** 4 servings (serving size: 2 lamb chops, about ½ cup skordalia, about 1 teaspoon pan juices, and 1 lemon wedge).

Per serving: CALORIES 285 (35% from fat); FAT 11.2g (saturated fat 3.5g); PROTEIN 31.2g; CARBOHYDRATES 13.7g; FIBER 1.1g; CHOLESTEROL 91mg; IRON 2.2mg; SODIUM 451mg; CALCIUM 75mg

Herbed Roasted Grape Tomatoes

prep: 6 minutes • **cook:** 13 minutes   *POINTS* value: 1

Preheat oven to 425°. Combine 2 pints grape tomatoes, 1 tablespoon chopped fresh basil, 1 tablespoon chopped fresh flat-leaf parsley, 1 teaspoons olive oil, ⅛ teaspoon salt, and ⅛ teaspoon freshly ground black pepper on a large rimmed baking sheet. Toss gently to coat. Bake at 425° for 13 minutes or until tomato skins pop, stirring after 8 minutes. **Yield:** 4 servings (serving size: ¾ cups).

Per serving: CALORIES 52 (48% from fat); FAT 2.8g (saturated fat 0.4g); PROTEIN 1.3g; CARBOHYDRATES 7g; FIBER 1.7g; CHOLESTEROL 0mg; IRON 0.8mg; SODIUM 87mg; CALCIUM 10mg

Pork Loin Chops with Lemon-Caper Sauce

prep: 4 minutes • **cook:** 10 minutes   *POINTS* value: 5

Be sure to measure and prepare all of the ingredients for the sauce before you begin to cook the garlic. The tangy sauce for the chops will take less than a minute to cook. To serve, spoon over hot cooked orzo.

2	teaspoons olive oil
4	(4-ounce) boneless center-cut loin pork chops (½ inch thick)
¼	teaspoon salt
¼	teaspoon freshly ground black pepper
2	cloves garlic, minced
¼	cup white wine
2	tablespoons fresh lemon juice
1	teaspoon grated lemon rind
2	tablespoons chopped fresh flat-leaf parsley
1	tablespoon capers, drained

1. Heat oil in a large nonstick skillet over medium-high heat. Sprinkle pork with salt and pepper. Add pork to pan; cook 4 to 5 minutes on each side or until done. Remove from pan, and keep warm.
2. Add garlic to pan; cook 30 seconds. Add wine; cook 15 seconds, stirring constantly to loosen browned bits from bottom of pan. Stir in lemon juice. Return pork to pan, and sprinkle with lemon rind, parsley, and capers. Serve immediately.
Yield: 4 servings (serving size: 1 pork chop and about 2 tablespoons sauce).

Per serving: CALORIES 198 (40% from fat); FAT 8.8g (saturated fat 2.7g); PROTEIN 24.1g; CARBOHYDRATES 1.9g; FIBER 0.3g; CHOLESTEROL 65mg; IRON 0.9mg; SODIUM 258mg; CALCIUM 32mg

Asparagus with Lemon and Garlic

prep: 3 minutes • **cook:** 3 minutes   *POINTS* value: 0

Preheat broiler. Combine 1 pound trimmed asparagus, 1 minced garlic clove, ½ teaspoon olive oil, ⅛ teaspoon salt, and ⅛ teaspoon freshly ground black pepper on a large rimmed baking sheet coated with cooking spray; toss gently to coat. Broil 3 minutes or until crisp-tender. Sprinkle with ½ teaspoon grated lemon rind; toss well. Serve immediately. **Yield:** 4 servings (serving size: ¼ of asparagus).

Per serving: CALORIES 35 (18% from fat); FAT 0.7g (saturated fat 0.1g); PROTEIN 2.6g; CARBOHYDRATES 4.7g; FIBER 2.4g; CHOLESTEROL 0mg; IRON 2.5mg; SODIUM 75mg; CALCIUM 29mg

---

Menu
POINTS value
per serving: 7

Pork Loin Chops with Lemon-Caper Sauce

Asparagus with Lemon and Garlic

½ cup cooked orzo
POINTS value: 2

Game Plan

1. While broiler preheats:
- Bring water for pasta to a boil.
- Chop parsley, and mince garlic.
- Trim asparagus.
- Zest and juice lemon.

2. While pork cooks:
- Cook pasta.
- Prepare asparagus.

3. While asparagus cooks:
- Cook sauce for pork.

pictured on page 46

Ginger-Sesame Pork Chops

prep: 4 minutes • **cook:** 10 minutes   *POINTS* value: 5

Start with ginger preserves and a sesame vinaigrette to create an Asian-inspired glaze for this weeknight entrée. Bright green cilantro gives these chops a burst of fresh flavor.

   3   tablespoons ginger preserves
   2   tablespoons reduced-fat Asian sesame vinaigrette (such as Newman's Own)
   2   tablespoons water
 Cooking spray
   4   (4-ounce) boneless center-cut loin pork chops (½ inch thick)
   1   tablespoon toasted sesame seeds
   ¼   cup fresh cilantro leaves

1. Combine preserves, vinaigrette, and water in a small bowl, stirring with a whisk; set aside.
2. Heat a large nonstick skillet over medium-high heat. Coat pan with cooking spray. Add pork chops to pan; cook 4 to 5 minutes on each side or until done. Remove pork chops from pan, and keep warm.
3. Add reserved preserves mixture to pan; cook over medium heat 1 minute or until syrupy. Spoon sauce over pork chops. Sprinkle each serving evenly with sesame seeds and cilantro leaves. **Yield:** 4 servings (serving size: 1 pork chop and 1½ tablespoon sauce).

Per serving: CALORIES 218 (32% from fat); FAT 7.7g (saturated fat 2.5g); PROTEIN 24.2g; CARBOHYDRATES 11.6g; FIBER 0.4g; CHOLESTEROL 65mg; IRON 0.9mg; SODIUM 146mg; CALCIUM 28mg

Hot Asian Noodle Salad

prep: 5 minutes • **cook:** 9 minutes   *POINTS* value: 2

Bring 4 ounces soba (buckwheat noodles) to a boil in a medium saucepan; cook 3 minutes or until tender but still firm. Add 1½ cups thinly sliced pretrimmed snow peas and ¾ cup matchstick-cut carrots to pan. Cook 1 minute or until crisp-tender. Drain and return to pan. Add 2 tablespoons reduced-fat Asian sesame vinaigrette (such as Newman's Own) and 3 tablespoons fresh cilantro leaves; toss gently to coat. **Yield:** 4 servings (serving size: about 1 cup).

Per serving: CALORIES 126 (6% from fat); FAT 0.9g (saturated fat 0g); PROTEIN 3.9g; CARBOHYDRATES 24.6g; FIBER 1.5g; CHOLESTEROL 0mg; IRON 0.6mg; SODIUM 255mg; CALCIUM 7mg

---

Menu
POINTS value
per serving: 7

Ginger-Sesame Pork Chops

Hot Asian Noodle Salad

Game Plan

1. While water comes to a boil for noodles:
  • Prepare preserves mixture for pork chops.
  • Slice snow peas.

2. While pork chops cook:
  • Toast sesame seeds.
  • Cook noodles, snow peas, and carrots.

3. While preserves mixture cooks:
  • Toss noodles and vegetables with vinaigrette.

Hoisin-Orange Pork Chops

prep: 3 minutes • **cook:** 8 minutes   *POINTS* value: 5

Perk up humble pork chops with a sweet hoisin sauce and aromatic Chinese five-spice powder—a blend of cinnamon, cloves, fennel seed, star anise, and Szechuan peppercorns. Precooked rice and steam-in-the-bag sugar snap peas help get this meal to the table in a snap.

    3 tablespoons hoisin sauce
    2 teaspoons grated orange rind
    1 teaspoon low-sodium soy sauce
    ¼ teaspoon five-spice powder
    4 (4-ounce) boneless center-cut loin pork chops (½ inch thick)
    1 teaspoon dark sesame oil
  Cooking spray

1. Preheat broiler.
2. Combine first 4 ingredients in a small bowl; stir with a whisk.
3. Rub pork chops with sesame oil, and baste with hoisin mixture. Place pork on a broiler pan coated with cooking spray, and cook 4 minutes on each side or until done, basting occasionally with remaining hoisin mixture. **Yield:** 4 servings (serving size: 1 pork chop).

Per serving: CALORIES 198 (37% from fat); FAT 8.1g (saturated fat 2.5g); PROTEIN 24.3g; CARBOHYDRATES 5.6g; FIBER 0.1g; CHOLESTEROL 65mg; IRON 0.7mg; SODIUM 279mg; CALCIUM 26mg

Coconut Rice

prep: 3 minutes • **cook:** 6 minutes   *POINTS* value: 2

Microwave 1 (8.8-ounce) microwaveable pouch cooked whole grain brown rice (such as Uncle Ben's) according to package directions. While rice cooks, heat a small nonstick skillet over medium-high heat. Add ¼ cup sweetened coconut flakes to pan; cook 2 minutes or until golden brown, stirring constantly. Remove coconut, and set aside. Return pan to medium-high heat; coat pan with cooking spray. Add ½ cup diced red bell pepper to pan; cook 2 minutes or until crisp-tender. Combine coconut, rice, and bell pepper in a medium bowl; toss well. **Yield:** 4 servings (serving size: ½ cup).

Per serving: CALORIES 124 (23% from fat); FAT 3.1g (saturated fat 1.5g); PROTEIN 2.6g; CARBOHYDRATES 21.8g; FIBER 1.7g; CHOLESTEROL 0mg; IRON 0.5mg; SODIUM 16mg; CALCIUM 2mg

---

Menu
POINTS value
per serving: 7

Hoisin-Orange Pork Chops

Coconut Rice

½ cup steamed
sugar snap peas
POINTS value: 0

Game Plan

1. While broiler preheats:
   • Prepare hoisin mixture
     for pork.

2. While pork cooks:
   • Cook rice.

3. While rice cooks:
   • Toast coconut.
   • Cook bell pepper.

4. While peas cook:
   • Toss rice with coconut and
     bell pepper.

Menu
POINTS value
per serving: 5

Rosemary Pork Chops

Apple and Cabbage Slaw

Game Plan

1. Chop rosemary; slice cabbage, apple, and green onion.

2. Season pork.

3. While pork cooks:
   • Prepare slaw.

Rosemary Pork Chops

prep: 3 minutes • **cook:** 7 minutes   *POINTS* value: 4

This five-ingredient pork chop recipe is a breeze to prepare. The pork's natural sweetness is complemented by the fruity and slightly acidic slaw, resulting in a tasty dish. To quickly remove the rosemary leaves from the stem, run your fingers along the stem in the opposite direction from which the leaves grow.

  1   teaspoon olive oil
  4   (4-ounce) boneless center-cut loin pork chops ($\frac{1}{2}$ inch thick)
  1   tablespoon fresh chopped rosemary
  $\frac{1}{4}$ teaspoon salt
  $\frac{1}{8}$ teaspoons black pepper

1. Heat oil in a large nonstick skillet over medium-high heat. Rub pork with rosemary, salt, and pepper. Add pork to pan; cook 3 minutes on each side or until done. **Yield:** 4 servings (serving size: 1 pork chop).

Per serving: CALORIES 171 (40% from fat); FAT 7.6g (saturated fat 2.5g); PROTEIN 23.9g; CARBOHYDRATES 0.3g; FIBER 0g; CHOLESTEROL 65mg; IRON 0.8mg; SODIUM 193mg; CALCIUM 30mg

Apple and Cabbage Slaw

prep: 7 minutes   *POINTS* value: 1

Combine 1 tablespoon cider vinegar, 1 tablespoon maple syrup, 2 teaspoons olive oil, $\frac{1}{4}$ teaspoon salt, and $\frac{1}{8}$ teaspoon black pepper in a large bowl, stirring with a whisk. Add 2 cups thinly sliced red cabbage, 1 cored and thinly sliced large Granny Smith apple, and 1 thinly sliced green onion to bowl; toss gently to coat. **Yield:** 4 servings (serving size: about 1 cup).

Per serving: CALORIES 76 (28% from fat); FAT 2.4g (saturated fat 0.3g); PROTEIN 0.8g; CARBOHYDRATES 14.6g; FIBER 2.1g; CHOLESTEROL 0mg; IRON 0.5mg; SODIUM 157mg; CALCIUM 26mg

Pork Chops with Tomatoes

prep: 2 minutes • **cook:** 18 minutes   *POINTS* value: 5

Proof that simple foods are often the best, this dish of pan-roasted grape tomatoes and juicy pork chops smells almost as good as it tastes. Serve this saucy entrée over creamy, cheesy grits for a down-home meal that you'll prepare over and over again.

   4   (4-ounce) boneless center-cut loin pork chops (about ½ inch thick)
   ½   teaspoon salt, divided
   ¼   teaspoon black pepper, divided
   2   teaspoons olive oil
   1   cup chopped onion
   1   tablespoon all-purpose flour
   1   cup fat-free, less-sodium beef broth
   1   pint grape tomatoes
   ½   teaspoon dried basil
   ½   teaspoon dried thyme
   ¼   teaspoon garlic powder

1. Preheat oven to 350°.
2. Sprinkle pork evenly with ¼ teaspoon salt and ⅛ teaspoon pepper.
3. Heat oil in a large cast-iron or ovenproof skillet over medium-high heat. Add pork chops to pan; cook 2 to 3 minutes on each side or until browned. Remove from pan, and keep warm.
4. Add onion to pan, and cook 2 minutes or until tender. Sprinkle flour evenly over onion, and cook 30 seconds, stirring constantly. Stir in broth, remaining ¼ teaspoon salt, remaining ⅛ teaspoon pepper, tomatoes, basil, thyme, and garlic powder. Bring to a boil; reduce heat, and simmer 1 minute, uncovered. Return pork chops to pan.
5. Bake at 350° for 8 minutes or until done. **Yield:** 4 servings (serving size: 1 pork chop and about ⅔ cup sauce).

Per serving: CALORIES 225 (36% from fat); FAT 9.1g (saturated fat 2.8g); PROTEIN 25.8g; CARBOHYDRATES 9.4g; FIBER 1.9g; CHOLESTEROL 65mg; IRON 1.4mg; SODIUM 457mg; CALCIUM 51mg

Cheese Grits

prep: 1 minute • **cook:** 6 minutes   *POINTS* value: 3

Bring 2 cups water to a boil in a medium saucepan over medium-high heat. Reduce heat to low; slowly add 4 (1-ounce) packets instant grits to pan, stirring constantly with a whisk. Add ½ cup reduced-fat shredded sharp Cheddar cheese and ⅛ teaspoon garlic powder; stir until thickened. **Yield:** 4 servings (serving size: about ½ cup).

Per serving: CALORIES 147 (18% from fat); FAT 3g (saturated fat 2g); PROTEIN 5.5g; CARBOHYDRATES 22.8g; FIBER 2g; CHOLESTEROL 10mg; IRON 8.2mg; SODIUM 444mg; CALCIUM 100mg

Menu
POINTS value
per serving: 8

Pork Chops with Tomatoes

Cheese Grits

Game Plan

1. While oven preheats:
   • Chop onion.
   • Brown pork in skillet.

2. While water for grits comes to a boil:
   • Cook broth mixture.

3. While pork cooks in oven:
   • Prepare grits.

pictured on page 43

Jerk-Seasoned Pork Tenderloin

prep: 3 minutes • **cook:** 12 minutes   *POINTS* value: 3

Menu
POINTS value
per serving: 6

Jerk-Seasoned Pork Tenderloin

Yellow Rice with Black Beans

½ cup lemon sorbet
POINTS value: 2

Butterflying the pork tenderloin helps it cook faster and creates more of a surface area to soak up the jerk seasoning. To butterfly, cut evenly down the center of the tenderloin without cutting all the way through.

Game Plan

1. While grill heats:
 • Season tenderloin.
 • Chop green onions, and mince garlic.
 • Cook rice.
 • Rinse and drain beans.

2. While tenderloin cooks:
 • Chop cilantro for salsa and rice.
 • Combine cilantro and salsa.

3. Toss rice with beans, lime juice, and cumin.

 1 (1-pound) pork tenderloin, butterflied
 2 teaspoons Caribbean jerk seasoning (such as McCormick's)
 ¼ teaspoon salt
 Cooking spray
 ½ cup fresh mango and peach salsa (such as Chachie's)
 1 tablespoon chopped fresh cilantro

1. Prepare grill.
2. Rub pork with jerk seasoning and salt. Place on a grill rack coated with cooking spray; grill 6 minutes on each side or until a thermometer registers 160° (slightly pink). Cut pork diagonally into slices.
3. While pork cooks, combine salsa and cilantro. Serve with pork. **Yield:** 4 servings (serving size: 3 ounces pork and 2 tablespoons salsa).

Per serving: CALORIES 151 (23% from fat); FAT 3.9g (saturated fat 1.3g); PROTEIN 22.5g; CARBOHYDRATES 5g; FIBER 0g; CHOLESTEROL 63mg; IRON 1.2mg; SODIUM 425mg; CALCIUM 5mg

Yellow Rice with Black Beans

prep: 2 minutes • **cook:** 16 minutes   *POINTS* value: 1

Heat a large nonstick skillet over medium-high heat. Coat pan with cooking spray. Add 2 chopped green onions and 1 minced garlic clove to pan. Sauté 1 to 2 minutes or until tender. Add 1 (3.5-ounce) bag boil-in-bag long-grain rice to pan. Add ½ teaspoon turmeric, and sauté 1 minute. Stir in ¾ cup fat-free, less-sodium chicken broth, ½ cup water, and ⅛ teaspoon salt; bring to a boil. Cover, reduce heat, and simmer 12 minutes or until rice is tender and liquid is absorbed. Stir in 1 cup rinsed and drained canned black beans, 1 tablespoon fresh lime juice, and ¼ teaspoon ground cumin. Sprinkle each serving with fresh chopped cilantro, if desired. **Yield:** 4 servings (serving size: about ½ cup).

Per serving: CALORIES 69 (1% from fat); FAT 0.1g (saturated fat 0g); PROTEIN 3.7g; CARBOHYDRATES 15.6g; FIBER 3.2g; CHOLESTEROL 0mg; IRON 1.3mg; SODIUM 287mg; CALCIUM 27mg

Poultry

Menu
POINTS value
per serving: 6

**Cumin-Rubbed Grilled Chicken
with Nectarine Salsa**

Lemony Couscous

Game Plan

1. While grill heats:
- Bring broth for couscous to a boil.
- Chop nectarine, red onion, mint, and green onions.
- Prepare couscous.

2. While couscous stands:
- Prepare spice mixture.
- Pound chicken, and rub with spice mixture.

3. While chicken cooks:
- Fluff couscous, and toss with lemon rind.
- Prepare salsa.

pictured on cover

Cumin-Rubbed Grilled Chicken with Nectarine Salsa

prep: 8 minutes • **cook:** 10 minutes   *POINTS* value: 4

Ripe, juicy freestone nectarines—the variety in which the pit easily pulls away from the fruit—are the key to quickly preparing the salsa. Look for them at your supermarket or at your local produce stand in late June when they are in season.

  1 teaspoon ground cumin
  1 teaspoon garlic powder
  1 teaspoon paprika
  ¼ teaspoon salt
  ¼ teaspoon black pepper
  4 (6-ounce) skinless, boneless chicken breast halves
Cooking spray
  1 cup chopped nectarines (about 1)
  ⅛ teaspoon salt
  3 tablespoons finely chopped red onion
  1 tablespoon chopped fresh mint
  1 tablespoon fresh lime juice

1. Prepare grill.
2. Combine cumin, garlic powder, paprika, ¼ teaspoon salt, and pepper in a bowl.
3. Place chicken breast halves between 2 sheets of heavy-duty plastic wrap; pound to ½-inch thickness using a meat mallet or small heavy skillet. Rub both sides of chicken evenly with spice mixture.
4. Place chicken on a grill rack coated with cooking spray; grill 5 minutes on each side or until done.
5. While chicken cooks, combine nectarines, ⅛ teaspoon salt, and remaining 3 ingredients in a small bowl; toss gently to coat. Serve salsa with chicken.
Yield: 4 servings (serving size: 1 chicken breast half and about ¼ cup salsa).

Per serving: CALORIES 214 (10% from fat); FAT 2.4g (saturated fat 0.6g); PROTEIN 40g; CARBOHYDRATES 6.1g; FIBER 1.1g; CHOLESTEROL 99mg; IRON 1.6mg; SODIUM 331mg; CALCIUM 28mg

Lemony Couscous

prep: 3 minutes • **cook:** 3 minutes • **other:** 5 minutes   *POINTS* value: 2

Combine 1 cup less-sodium chicken stock (such as Swanson's) and ⅛ teaspoon black pepper in a small saucepan over medium-high heat; cover, and bring to a boil. Stir in ⅔ cup couscous, ¼ cup golden raisins, and ¼ cup chopped green onions. Remove pan from heat; cover, and let stand 5 minutes. Fluff with a fork and stir in 2 teaspoons grated lemon rind. **Yield:** 4 servings (serving size: about ⅔ cup).

Per serving: CALORIES 143 (1% from fat); FAT 0.2g (saturated fat 0.1g); PROTEIN 5.1g; CARBOHYDRATES 30.4g; FIBER 2.1g; CHOLESTEROL 0mg; IRON 0.6mg; SODIUM 133mg; CALCIUM 18mg

Grilled Chicken with Bell Peppers and Onions

prep: 8 minutes • **cook:** 10 minutes   *POINTS* value: 5

Grilled bell peppers and onions marry well with pungent balsamic vinegar and fragrant rosemary. For a variation, try substituting pork chops or steak for the chicken.

  6 (4-ounce) skinless, boneless chicken breast halves
  ½ teaspoon salt
  ½ teaspoon freshly ground black pepper
Cooking spray
  1 small red bell pepper, halved and seeded
  1 small yellow bell pepper, halved and seeded
  1 small green bell pepper, halved and seeded
  1 medium onion, cut into 4 (½-inch) slices
  1 tablespoon chopped fresh rosemary
  3 tablespoons balsamic vinegar
  1 teaspoon olive oil
  1 garlic clove, minced

1. Prepare grill.

2. Place chicken breast halves between 2 sheets of heavy-duty plastic wrap; pound to ½-inch thickness using a meat mallet or small heavy skillet. Sprinkle chicken evenly with salt and black pepper.

3. Place chicken, bell peppers, and onion on grill rack coated with cooking spray. Grill 5 minutes on each side or until chicken is done and vegetables are tender. Slice bell peppers into ¼-inch-thick strips, and cut onion slices in half. Combine peppers, onion, and remaining ingredients in a medium bowl; toss gently to coat. Serve vegetable mixture with chicken. **Yield:** 4 servings (serving size: 1 chicken breast half and ¾ cup vegetable mixture).

Per serving: CALORIES 244 (14% from fat); FAT 3.5g (saturated fat 0.8g); PROTEIN 40g; CARBOHYDRATES 5.7g; FIBER 1.2g; CHOLESTEROL 99mg; IRON 1.6mg; SODIUM 406mg; CALCIUM 31mg

pictured on page 47

Chicken with Pine Nut Gremolata

Game Plan

1. While water for pasta comes to a boil:
- Chop tomato, and prepare tomato mixture for pasta.
- Pound chicken; season with salt and pepper.

2. While pasta cooks:
- Cook chicken.
- Prepare gremolata.

3. Toss pasta with tomato mixture.

prep: 3 minutes • **cook:** 11 minutes   *POINTS* value: 5

Gremolata, an Italian garnish made of minced parsley, lemon rind, and garlic, is a good companion to versatile chicken breasts. For a company-worthy presentation, plate the chicken and gremolata on top of a colorful bed of Orzo and Tomatoes (see recipe below).

4   (6-ounce) skinless, boneless chicken breast halves
½   teaspoon salt
⅛   teaspoon freshly ground black pepper
2   teaspoons olive oil, divided
1   cup loosely packed fresh flat-leaf parsley, finely chopped
2   tablespoons pine nuts
1   garlic clove, minced
½   teaspoon grated lemon rind
1   tablespoon fresh lemon juice
⅛   teaspoon salt
1/16 teaspoon freshly ground black pepper

1. Place chicken breast halves between 2 sheets of heavy-duty plastic wrap; pound to ½-inch thickness using a meat mallet or a small heavy skillet. Sprinkle chicken with ½ teaspoon salt and ⅛ teaspoon pepper.
2. Heat 1 teaspoon oil in a large nonstick skillet over medium-high heat. Add chicken to pan, and cook 5 minutes on each side or until done.
3. While chicken cooks, combine parsley, pine nuts, remaining 1 teaspoon olive oil, garlic, and next 4 ingredients in a small bowl; toss gently to coat. Serve gremolata over chicken. **Yield:** 4 servings (serving size: 1 chicken breast half and about 1½ tablespoons gremolata).

Per serving: CALORIES 244 (28% from fat); FAT 7.5g (saturated fat 1.1g); PROTEIN 40g; CARBOHYDRATES 2.2g; FIBER 0.7g; CHOLESTEROL 99mg; IRON 2.4mg; SODIUM 483mg; CALCIUM 43mg

Orzo and Tomatoes

prep: 1 minute • **cook:** 16 minutes   *POINTS* value: 2

Combine 5 cups water and ¼ teaspoon salt in a large saucepan; cover, and bring to a boil. Add ¾ cup (5 ounces) orzo (rice-shaped pasta) to pan, and cook 11 minutes or until tender; drain. While water for pasta comes to a boil, combine ¾ cup chopped tomato, ½ teaspoon olive oil, and ⅛ teaspoon black pepper in a medium bowl. Add orzo to tomato mixture; toss gently to coat. **Yield:** 4 servings (serving size: about ½ cup).

Per serving: CALORIES 127 (9% from fat); FAT 1.2g (saturated fat 0.1g); PROTEIN 4.2g; CARBOHYDRATES 24.6; FIBER 1.4g; CHOLESTEROL 0mg; IRON 0.1mg; SODIUM 146mg; CALCIUM 3mg

Chicken Saté with Salsa Verde Sauce

prep: 7 minutes • **cook:** 6 minutes   *POINTS* value: 4

Tangy salsa verde, a green salsa made from tomatillos, is commonly used in Latin cuisines. Look for salsa verde on the ethnic or organic food aisle at your local supermarket.

  ¾   cup bottled salsa verde (such as Zapata)
  1   teaspoon reduced-fat sour cream
1½   teaspoons chopped fresh cilantro
  ⅓   cup fresh lime juice
  4   (6-ounce) skinless, boneless chicken breast halves, cut into thin strips
1½   teaspoons ground cumin
  ⅛   teaspoon salt
  ¼   teaspoon freshly ground black pepper
    Cooking spray

1. Prepare grill.
2. Combine salsa verde, sour cream, and cilantro in a small bowl. Cover and chill until ready to serve.
3. Drizzle lime juice over chicken; sprinkle evenly with cumin, salt, and pepper. Thread chicken onto 8 (10-inch) metal skewers. Place skewers on grill rack coated with cooking spray; grill 3 to 4 minutes on each side or until done. Serve with chilled salsa verde mixture. **Yield:** 4 servings (serving size: 2 skewers and 3 tablespoons sauce).

Per serving: CALORIES 213 (11% from fat); FAT 2.5g (saturated fat 0.7g); PROTEIN 39.6g; CARBOHYDRATES 5.2g; FIBER 0.4g; CHOLESTEROL 99mg; IRON 1.5mg; SODIUM 336mg; CALCIUM 31mg

Cilantro-Lime Rice

prep: 3 minutes • **cook:** 2 minutes   *POINTS* value: 2

Microwave 1 (8.8-ounce) pouch microwaveable cooked whole grain brown rice (such as Uncle Ben's) according to package directions. Combine rice, 2 tablespoons chopped fresh cilantro, 2 tablespoons lime juice, and ¼ teaspoon salt in a medium bowl; toss well. **Yield:** 4 servings (serving size: about ½ cup).

Per serving: CALORIES 100 (16% from fat); FAT 1.8g (saturated fat 0.2g); PROTEIN 2.3g; CARBOHYDRATES 18.9g; FIBER 0.9g; CHOLESTEROL 0mg; IRON 0.3mg; SODIUM 148mg; CALCIUM 2mg

---

Menu
POINTS value
per serving: 6

**Chicken Saté
with Salsa Verde Sauce**

Cilantro-Lime Rice

Game Plan

1. While grill heats:
  • Chop cilantro, and juice limes for chicken and rice.
  • Prepare salsa verde mixture.
  • Season chicken.

2. While chicken cooks:
  • Heat rice in microwave.

3. Toss rice with cilantro and lime juice.

Menu
POINTS value
per serving: 7

**Chicken with
Tomato-Caper Salsa**

½ cup angel hair pasta tossed
with chopped fresh parsley
POINTS value: 2

Game Plan

1. While water for pasta comes to
a boil:
- Pound chicken, and sprinkle
  with breadcrumbs.
- Chop parsley; dice tomato
  and zucchini.

2. While chicken cooks:
- Cook pasta.
- Prepare salsa.

3. Toss pasta with parsley.

Chicken with Tomato-Caper Salsa

prep: 3 minutes • **cook:** 12 minutes   *POINTS* value: 5

**Fresh salsa plus a few garden vegetables create a winning topping
for succulent chicken breasts. Capers and olives lend a distinctive
Mediterranean flair.**

  4   (6-ounce) skinless, boneless chicken breast halves
  2   tablespoons Italian-seasoned breadcrumbs
  2   teaspoons olive oil
  2   tablespoons water
  ¾   cup refrigerated fresh salsa
  ⅓   cup diced plum tomato
  ⅓   cup diced zucchini
  2   tablespoons chopped ripe olives
  2   teaspoons capers

1. Place chicken breast halves between 2 sheets of heavy-duty plastic wrap; pound
to a ½-inch thickness using a meat mallet or small heavy skillet. Sprinkle chicken
with breadcrumbs.
2. Heat oil in a large nonstick skillet over medium-high heat. Add chicken to pan;
cook 2 minutes on each side or until browned. Reduce heat to low; add 2 tablespoons water to pan. Cover and cook 8 minutes or until done.
3. While chicken cooks, combine salsa and next 4 ingredients in a small bowl; toss
well. Serve salsa over chicken. **Yield:** 4 servings (serving size: 1 chicken breast half
and about ⅓ cup salsa).

Per serving: CALORIES 245 (19% from fat); FAT 5.1g (saturated fat 1g); PROTEIN 40.1g; CARBOHYDRATES 5.3g; FIBER 0.6g; CHOLESTEROL 99mg; IRON 1.6mg;
SODIUM 360mg; CALCIUM 31mg

pictured on page 113

Balsamic Chicken and Mushrooms

prep: 3 minutes • **cook:** 17 minutes   *POINTS* value: 3

Adding water to the mushrooms while they cook makes them tender and saucy. To cook the potatoes, microwave 4 (6-ounce) potatoes at HIGH for 8 to 9 minutes or until tender, rearranging after 5 minutes. Wrap the potatoes in a towel, and let stand for 5 minutes before serving.

    1   slice bacon, finely chopped
    ¾   pound chicken cutlets (about 4 cutlets)
    3   tablespoons balsamic vinegar, divided
    ¼   teaspoon salt, divided
    ¼   teaspoon freshly ground black pepper, divided
    1   (8-ounce) package presliced baby portobello mushrooms
    ½   cup sliced green onions
    1   tablespoon chopped fresh rosemary
    1   tablespoon water
    Rosemary sprigs (optional)

1. Heat a large nonstick skillet over medium-high heat. Add bacon to pan; cook 3 minutes or until crisp. Remove bacon from pan, and drain bacon on paper towel; set aside. Reserve drippings in pan.
2. Brush chicken with 1 tablespoon vinegar and sprinkle with ⅛ teaspoon salt and ⅛ teaspoon pepper. Add chicken to drippings in pan, and cook 3 minutes on each side or until done. Remove chicken from pan; keep warm.
3. Add mushrooms, green onions, and rosemary to pan. Cook, stirring frequently, 1 minute. Stir in water, remaining 2 tablespoons vinegar, remaining ⅛ teaspoon salt, and remaining ⅛ teaspoon pepper. Cook 6 minutes or until mushrooms are tender, stirring occasionally. Stir in bacon. Spoon mushroom mixture over chicken. Garnish with rosemary springs, if desired. **Yield:** 4 servings (serving size: about 1 chicken cutlet and about ⅓ cup mushroom mixture).

Per serving: CALORIES 150 (25% from fat); FAT 4.1g (saturated fat 1.4g); PROTEIN 22.3g; CARBOHYDRATES 5g; FIBER 1g; CHOLESTEROL 53mg; IRON 1.2mg; SODIUM 248mg; CALCIUM 26mg

Roasted Zucchini

prep: 2 minutes • **cook:** 13 minutes   *POINTS* value: 0

Preheat oven to 475°. Cut 4 medium zucchini in half crosswise; cut each half lengthwise into 4 slices. Toss zucchini with 2 teaspoons olive oil on a baking sheet. Bake at 475° for 13 minutes or until crisp-tender. Sprinkle zucchini with 1 tablespoon chopped fresh oregano, ¼ teaspoon salt, ¼ teaspoon freshly ground black pepper, and 1/16 teaspoon sugar; toss gently to coat. **Yield:** 4 servings (serving size: about 1 cup).

Per serving: CALORIES 53 (46% from fat); FAT 2.7g (saturated fat 0.4g); PROTEIN 2.4g; CARBOHYDRATES 6.9g; FIBER 2.2g; CHOLESTEROL 0mg; IRON 0.7mg; SODIUM 165mg; CALCIUM 35mg

---

Menu
POINTS value
per serving: 6

Balsamic Chicken and Mushrooms

Roasted Zucchini

1 (6-ounce) baked potato with 2 teaspoons light butter
POINTS value: 3

Game Plan

1. While oven preheats:
  • Cook bacon.
  • Slice zucchini.
  • Prepare chicken.

2. While chicken cooks:
  • Cook zucchini.
  • Chop rosemary and oregano; slice green onions.
  • Cook potatoes in microwave, and let stand.

3. Cook mushroom mixture.

pictured on page 48

Chicken Cutlets with Fontina and Fresh Blueberry Sauce

prep: 5 minutes • **cook:** 10 minutes

POINTS value: 4

Buttery fontina cheese and a sweet-savory, jewel-toned blueberry sauce turn modest chicken cutlets into an extraordinary dish that family and friends will love.

Menu
POINTS value
per serving: 7

Chicken Cutlets with Fontina and Fresh Blueberry Sauce

Ginger-Roasted Green Beans

1 (1.3-ounce) dinner roll
POINTS value: 2

Game Plan

1. While oven preheats:
- Grate ginger, mince thyme, and shred cheese.

2. While green beans cook:
- Cook chicken.
- Cook blueberry sauce.
- Warm dinner rolls.

1   tablespoon butter, divided
¾   pound chicken cutlets (about 4 cutlets)
½   teaspoon salt
¼   teaspoon freshly ground black pepper
½   cup (2 ounces) shredded fontina cheese
3   tablespoons apple juice
1   tablespoon rice wine vinegar
½   teaspoon Dijon mustard
1   cup fresh blueberries
1½   teaspoons minced fresh thyme

1. Melt 1 teaspoon butter in a large nonstick skillet over medium-high heat. Sprinkle chicken with salt and pepper. Add chicken to pan; cook 3 minutes on each side or until done. Remove chicken to a platter; sprinkle with cheese. Keep warm.
2. Combine apple juice, vinegar, and mustard in a small bowl; stir well with a whisk. Add apple juice mixture to pan; simmer 1 minute. Add blueberries and thyme; simmer 2 minutes. Stir in remaining 2 teaspoons butter. Spoon blueberry sauce over chicken. **Yield:** 4 servings (serving size: about 1 chicken cutlet and 2 tablespoons sauce).

Per serving: CALORIES 199 (37% from fat); FAT 8.2g (saturated fat 4.7g); PROTEIN 23.4g; CARBOHYDRATES 7.2g; FIBER 1g; CHOLESTEROL 73mg; IRON 0.8mg; SODIUM 491mg; CALCIUM 89mg

Ginger-Roasted Green Beans

prep: 2 minutes • **cook:** 10 minutes

POINTS value: 1

Preheat oven to 450°. Combine 1 (12-ounce) package pretrimmed green beans, 2 teaspoons olive oil, 2 teaspoons grated peeled fresh ginger, and ⅛ teaspoon salt on a baking sheet; toss well. Spread beans in a single layer. Bake at 450° for 10 minutes or until crisp-tender. **Yield:** 4 servings (serving size: about ¾ cup).

Per serving: CALORIES 47 (46% from fat); FAT 2.4g (saturated fat 0.4g); PROTEIN 1.6g; CARBOHYDRATES 62g; FIBER 2.9g; CHOLESTEROL 0mg; IRON 0.9mg; SODIUM 78mg; CALCIUM 32mg

Herbed Chicken Cutlets

prep: 5 minutes • **cook:** 7 minutes   *POINTS* value: 5

Look in your pantry and you'll probably find the medley of dried herbs you'll need to prepare this quick entrée. Peppery arugula tossed with a simple, homemade vinaigrette and a dessert of fresh mixed melon complete this easy menu.

1½ pounds chicken cutlets (about 8 cutlets)
½   teaspoon dried tarragon
½   teaspoon dried basil
½   teaspoon dried thyme
½   teaspoon salt
¼   teaspoon black pepper
1   tablespoon olive oil

1. Sprinkle chicken evenly with tarragon and next 4 ingredients.
2. Heat oil in a large nonstick skillet over medium-high heat. Add chicken to pan, and cook 3 minutes on each side or until done. **Yield:** 4 servings (serving size: about 2 chicken cutlets).

Per serving: CALORIES 219 (24% from fat); FAT 5.6g (saturated fat 1.1g); PROTEIN 39.4g; CARBOHYDRATES 0.4g; FIBER 0.2g; CHOLESTEROL 99mg; IRON 1.5mg; SODIUM 402mg; CALCIUM 28mg

Arugula Salad

prep: 7 minutes   *POINTS* value: 1

Combine 4 teaspoons white wine vinegar, 1 tablespoon water, 1 tablespoon olive oil, 1 tablespoon minced shallots, ¼ teaspoon salt, and ¼ teaspoon black pepper in a large bowl. Add 1 (5-ounce) package arugula to bowl; toss well. Serve immediately. **Yield:** 4 servings (serving size: 1¼ cups).

Per serving: CALORIES 42 (79% from fat); FAT 3.7g (saturated fat 0.5g); PROTEIN 1g; CARBOHYDRATES 2.1g; FIBER 0.6g; CHOLESTEROL 0mg; IRON 0.6mg; SODIUM 155mg; CALCIUM 58mg

---

Menu
POINTS value
per serving: 7

Herbed Chicken Cutlets

Arugula Salad

1 cup prechopped mixed melon
POINTS value: 1

Game Plan

1. Season chicken with herb mixture.

2. While chicken cooks:
• Prepare salad.

---

pictured on page 114

Chicken with Peanut Sauce and Lo Mein Noodles

prep: 2 minutes • **cook:** 18 minutes

POINTS value: 8

Wide lo mein noodles capture the spicy peanut sauce in this Thai-inspired one-dish meal. Linguine or fettuccine pasta can be substituted.

Menu
POINTS value
per serving: 8

**Chicken with Peanut Sauce
and Lo Mein Noodles**

Game Plan

1. While water for noodles comes to a boil:
 • Chop basil and peanuts; mince garlic, and grate ginger.

2. While noodles cook:
 • Prepare chicken and vegetable mixture.

3. Toss noodles with chicken and vegetable mixture; top with basil and peanuts.

 8 ounces wide lo mein noodles
 1 (14-ounce) can fat-free, less-sodium chicken broth
 ⅓ cup reduced-fat peanut butter
 2 tablespoons rice vinegar
 2 tablespoons sweet chili sauce (such as Maggi)
 2 tablespoons low-sodium soy sauce
 2 teaspoons dark sesame oil, divided
Cooking spray
 1 pound chicken breast tenders, cut in half
 2 teaspoons minced garlic
 1 teaspoon grated ginger
 1 (18-ounce) package fresh vegetable stir-fry vegetable medley (about 6 cups)
 3 tablespoons chopped fresh basil
 2 tablespoons chopped unsalted, dry-roasted peanuts

1. Cook lo mein noodles according to package directions, omitting salt and fat; drain.
2. Combine chicken broth and next 4 ingredients in a small bowl; stir well with a whisk. Set aside.
3. While lo mein noodles cook, heat 1 teaspoon oil in a large, deep nonstick skillet coated with cooking spray over medium-high heat. Add chicken to pan; sauté 6 minutes or until done. Remove from pan, and set aside.
4. Add remaining 1 teaspoon oil to pan. Add garlic and ginger to pan; sauté 30 seconds. Add vegetable mix to pan; sauté 4 minutes or just until crisp-tender. Stir in peanut butter mixture. Bring to boil over medium-high heat; cook 5 minutes or until thick. Return chicken to pan; cook 2 minutes or until chicken is thoroughly heated. Add noodles; toss well. Top each serving with chopped basil and peanuts.
Yield: 6 servings (serving size: about 2 cups chicken mixture, 1½ teaspoons basil, and 1 teaspoon peanuts).

Per serving: CALORIES 374 (23% from fat); FAT 9.5g (saturated fat 1.8g); PROTEIN 26.3g; CARBOHYDRATES 46g; FIBER 3.6g; CHOLESTEROL 44mg; IRON 2.3mg; SODIUM 628mg; CALCIUM 73mg

Five-Spice Chicken and Vegetable Stir-Fry

prep: 6 minutes • **cook:** 10 minutes   *POINTS* value: 6

A package of prechopped fresh stir-fry vegetables jump-starts this weeknight meal. Once the other ingredients for this recipe are prepped, the cooking goes quickly, so have everything ready before you heat the pan. Serve the stir-fry atop Almond Rice (see recipe below).

¼	cup fat-free, less-sodium chicken broth
2	tablespoons hoisin sauce
2	tablespoons low-sodium soy sauce
2	teaspoons rice vinegar
2	teaspoons cornstarch
½	teaspoon chili sauce with garlic (such as Hokan)
1½	pounds chicken tenders, cut into thin strips
1	teaspoon five-spice powder
4	teaspoons canola oil, divided
2	tablespoons minced fresh ginger
1	(12-ounce) package fresh vegetable stir-fry medley (about 4 cups)
1	tablespoon water

1. Combine first 6 ingredients in a small bowl; set aside. Toss chicken with five-spice powder.
2. Heat 2 teaspoons oil in a large nonstick skillet over medium-high heat. Add ginger to pan; cook 30 seconds. Add chicken to pan; cook 5 minutes or until done. Remove chicken from pan; keep warm.
3. Add remaining 2 teaspoons oil to pan. Add vegetables and water to pan; cook 3 minutes or until vegetables are crisp-tender. Return chicken to pan. Pour chicken broth mixture over chicken and vegetables; cook, stirring constantly, 1 minute or until sauce thickens. **Yield:** 4 servings (serving size: 1¼ cups).

Per serving: CALORIES 276 (24% from fat); FAT 7.3g (saturated fat 0.9g); PROTEIN 41.2g; CARBOHYDRATES 9.7g; FIBER 1.2g; CHOLESTEROL 99mg; IRON 1.8mg; SODIUM 576mg; CALCIUM 86mg

Almond Rice

prep: 2 minutes • **cook:** 2 minutes   *POINTS* value: 2

Microwave 1 (8.8-ounce) pouch microwaveable cooked long-grain brown rice (such as Uncle Ben's) according to package directions. Combine rice, 2 tablespoons sliced almonds, and ¼ teaspoon salt in a medium bowl; toss well. Serve immediately. **Yield:** 4 servings (serving size: ½ cup).

Per serving: CALORIES 115 (26% from fat); FAT 3.3g (saturated fat 0.3g); PROTEIN 2.9g; CARBOHYDRATES 18.9g; FIBER 1.2g; CHOLESTEROL 0mg; IRON 0.5mg; SODIUM 148mg; CALCIUM 7mg

Game Plan

1. Prepare chicken broth mixture.

2. Cut chicken into strips; mince ginger.

3. While chicken and vegetable mixture cooks:
   • Heat rice in microwave.

4. Toss rice with almonds.

Menu
POINTS value
per serving: 8

Asian Barbecue Chicken

Zesty Broccoli Slaw

Game Plan

1. While grill heats:
- Prepare hoisin mixture for chicken.

2. While chicken marinates:
- Chop mint; grate ginger.

3. While chicken cooks:
- Toast sesame seeds.
- Prepare vinegar mixture for slaw.
- Toss slaw.

Asian Barbecue Chicken

prep: 3 minutes • **cook:** 10 minutes • **other:** 5 minutes   *POINTS* value: 8

Chinese hoisin sauce, mirin (a Japanese sweet rice wine), and Asian chili-garlic sauce create a quick, no-boil barbecue sauce that stands up to the dark meat of the chicken thighs.

¼ cup hoisin sauce
1½ tablespoons mirin (sweet rice wine)
1 teaspoon chile sauce with garlic (such as Hokan)
8 chicken thighs (about 2 pounds), skinned
Cooking spray
¼ cup presliced green onions

1. Prepare grill.
2. Combine first 3 ingredients in a large zip-top plastic bag; add chicken. Seal bag and marinate 5 minutes. Remove chicken, and discard bag.
3. Place chicken on grill rack coated with cooking spray; grill 5 minutes on each side or until done. Transfer chicken to a platter, and sprinkle with green onions. **Yield:** 4 servings (serving size: about 2 chicken thighs).

Per serving: CALORIES 321 (45% from fat); FAT 16.1g (saturated fat 4.2g); PROTEIN 31.7g; CARBOHYDRATES 8.8g; FIBER 0.2g; CHOLESTEROL 115mg; IRON 1.7mg; SODIUM 350mg; CALCIUM 19mg

Zesty Broccoli Slaw

prep: 7 minutes • **other:** 5 minutes   *POINTS* value: 0

Combine 2 tablespoons seasoned rice vinegar, 2 tablespoons fresh lime juice, 2 tablespoons chopped fresh mint, 1 tablespoon reduced-sodium soy sauce, and ½ teaspoon grated fresh ginger in a large bowl, stirring with a whisk. Add 2 cups broccoli slaw, 2 cups angel hair cabbage slaw, and ⅓ cup presliced green onions to bowl; toss gently to coat. Let stand 5 minutes. Sprinkle slaw with 2 teaspoons toasted sesame seeds; toss well. **Yield:** 4 servings (serving size: about 1 cup).

Per serving: CALORIES 37 (19% from fat); FAT 0.8g (saturated fat 0.1g); PROTEIN 1.6g; CARBOHYDRATES 6.5g; FIBER 1.9g; CHOLESTEROL 0mg; IRON 1mg; SODIUM 296mg; CALCIUM 45mg

Chicken Thighs with Quick Romesco Sauce

prep: 6 minutes • **cook:** 10 minutes   *POINTS* value: 7

For a traditional Spanish romesco sauce, the signature ingredients are tomatoes, red bell peppers, almonds, oil, and garlic. Here, we've simplified the sauce by using a few convenience items and reduced the fat by substituting store-bought croutons for the almonds. Long, thin Japanese eggplants have a firm flesh that is ideal for high-heat cooking methods, such as grilling, broiling, or pan-frying.

    8   chicken thighs (about 2 pounds), skinned
    3   tablespoons light balsamic vinaigrette, divided
    1   medium plum tomato, quartered
    1   bottled roasted red bell pepper, drained
    ½   cup croutons
Cooking spray
    ¼   cup chopped fresh basil

1. Prepare grill.
2. Combine chicken and 2 tablespoons vinaigrette in a medium bowl; toss gently to coat.
3. Place remaining 1 tablespoon vinaigrette and next 3 ingredients in a blender or food processor; process until smooth. Set aside.
4. Place chicken on grill rack coated with cooking spray; grill 5 minutes on each side or until done. Serve with romesco sauce, and sprinkle with basil. **Yield:** 4 servings (serving size: about 2 chicken thighs, about 3 tablespoons sauce, and 1 tablespoon basil).

Per serving: CALORIES 294 (47% from fat); FAT 15.3g (saturated fat 4g); PROTEIN 31.2g; CARBOHYDRATES 5.6g; FIBER 0.5g; CHOLESTEROL 112mg; IRON 1.8mg; SODIUM 417mg; CALCIUM 24mg

Grilled Eggplant

prep: 6 minutes • **cook:** 8 minutes • **other:** 3 minutes   *POINTS* value: 0

Prepare grill. Cut 3 Japanese eggplants lengthwise into thirds. Brush with 2 tablespoons light balsamic vinaigrette; let stand 3 to 5 minutes. Place eggplant on grill rack coated with cooking spray; grill 4 minutes on each side or until tender. **Yield:** 4 servings (serving size: about 2 slices).

Per serving: CALORIES 38 (28% from fat); FAT 1.2g (saturated fat 0.2g); PROTEIN 1.2g; CARBOHYDRATES 7g; FIBER 3.8g; CHOLESTEROL 0mg; IRON 0.3mg; SODIUM 120mg; CALCIUM 10mg

Menu
POINTS value
per serving: 7

Chicken Thighs with Quick Romesco Sauce

Grilled Eggplant

Game Plan

1. While grill heats:
  • Slice eggplant, brush with vinaigrette, and let stand.
  • Toss chicken with vinaigrette.

2. While chicken and eggplant cook:
  • Prepare romesco sauce.

Menu
POINTS value
per serving: 8

Curry-Chutney Chicken Thighs

Wasabi Peas

Game Plan

1. While broiler preheats:
 • Mince green onions.
 • Brush chicken with chutney mixture.

2. While chicken cooks:
 • Prepare peas.

Curry-Chutney Chicken Thighs

prep: 4 minutes • **cook:** 10 minutes   *POINTS* value: 7

When it comes to great chicken flavor, thighs can't be beat. Cheap and tasty, chicken thighs can be quick and easy to prepare, too. Jarred mango chutney—combined with curry powder, green onions, and a little salt—is all that's needed to concoct the spicy-sweet glaze.

⅓ cup mango chutney
1 tablespoon minced green onions
2 teaspoons curry powder
¼ teaspoon salt
8 chicken thighs (about 2 pounds), skinned
Cooking spray

1. Preheat broiler.
2. Combine first 4 ingredients in a medium bowl. Brush both sides of chicken with chutney mixture.
3. Place chicken on a broiler pan coated with cooking spray; broil 5 minutes on each side or until done. **Yield:** 4 servings (serving size: about 2 chicken thighs).

Per serving: CALORIES 302 (38% from fat); FAT 12.9g (saturated fat 3.6g); PROTEIN 30.6g; CARBOHYDRATES 12.7g; FIBER 0.4g; CHOLESTEROL 112mg; IRON 1.9mg; SODIUM 423mg; CALCIUM 20mg

Wasabi Peas

prep: 3 minutes • **cook:** 4 minutes   *POINTS* value: 1

Combine 1 (10-ounce) package frozen petite green peas and ¼ cup fat-free, less-sodium chicken broth in a medium saucepan; bring to a boil. Remove from heat. Stir in 2 teaspoons wasabi paste and ⅛ teaspoon salt. **Yield:** 4 servings (serving size: ½ cup).

Per serving: CALORIES 73 (6% from fat); FAT 0.5g (saturated fat 0.1g); PROTEIN 3.9g; CARBOHYDRATES 11.3g; FIBER 3g; CHOLESTEROL 0mg; IRON 1.1mg; SODIUM 250mg; CALCIUM 16mg

Turkey Cutlets with Cranberry Salsa

prep: 8 minutes • **cook:** 12 minutes   *POINTS* value: 5

Enjoy the flavors of Thanksgiving all year long with this vibrant menu of turkey, cranberries, and sweet potatoes. The cranberry salsa is also delicious on turkey sandwiches.

    1   medium orange
    ¾   cups fresh or frozen cranberries
    2   tablespoons coarsely chopped green onions
    2   tablespoons fresh mint leaves
    2   tablespoons honey
  1½   pounds turkey cutlets
    ½   teaspoon salt
    ¼   teaspoon freshly ground black pepper
Cooking spray
    2   teaspoons olive oil, divided
    ¼   cup low-sugar orange marmalade

1. Grate 1 tablespoon rind from orange; set grated rind aside.
2. Peel and section orange over food processor bowl to catch juices. Add grated orange rind, orange sections, cranberries, and next 3 ingredients; process until coarsely chopped, scraping down sides, if necessary.
3. Sprinkle turkey with salt and pepper; coat with cooking spray.
4. Heat 1 teaspoons oil in a large nonstick skillet over medium high heat. Add half of turkey to pan; cook 2 minutes on each side or until lightly browned; remove from pan. Keep warm. Repeat procedure with remaining 1 teaspoon oil and remaining turkey.
5. Add marmalade to pan; cook 2 minutes or until marmalade is melted. Return turkey to pan, turning to coat with marmalade. Serve with cranberry mixture.
Yield: 4 servings (serving size: about 2 turkey cutlets and about ¼ cup salsa).

Per serving: CALORIES 242 (12% from fat); FAT 3.1g (saturated fat 0.3g); PROTEIN 42.3g; CARBOHYDRATES 10.3g; FIBER 1g; CHOLESTEROL 68mg; IRON 2.3mg; SODIUM 441mg; CALCIUM 16mg

Menu
POINTS value
per serving: 7

Turkey Cutlets with Cranberry Salsa

½ **cup refrigerated mashed sweet potatoes**
POINTS value: 2

Game Plan

1. Prepare salsa.

2. While turkey cooks:
  • Cook sweet potatoes in microwave.

Menu
POINTS value
per serving: 6

Turkey Cutlets with Orange Sauce

Spinach Salad with Honey-Dijon
Vinaigrette

Game Plan

1. Sprinkle turkey with salt,
pepper, and cornstarch.

2. Cook turkey.

3. While orange juice mixture
cooks:
• Slice mushrooms.
• Prepare vinaigrette.

4. Toss salad.

Turkey Cutlets with Orange Sauce

prep: 4 minutes • **cook:** 12 minutes   **POINTS** value: 5

A dusting of cornstarch gives these cutlets a light crust that absorbs the sweet citrus sauce. Thin turkey cutlets cook very quickly, so be sure to watch them carefully.

1½ pounds turkey cutlets
½ teaspoon salt
¼ teaspoon black pepper
1 tablespoon cornstarch
2 teaspoons olive oil, divided
1 cup orange juice
1 teaspoon brown sugar
3 tablespoons raisins

1. Sprinkle both sides of turkey with salt and pepper. Place cornstarch in a small metal sieve; sprinkle both sides of turkey evenly with cornstarch.
2. Heat 1 teaspoon oil in a large nonstick skillet over medium-high heat; add half of turkey to pan. Cook 2 minutes on each side or until lightly browned; remove from pan. Keep warm. Repeat procedure with remaining 1 teaspoon olive oil and remaining turkey.
3. Add orange juice, brown sugar, and raisins to pan; bring to a boil over high heat, and boil 2 minutes.
4. Return turkey to pan, turning to coat with sauce. **Yield:** 4 servings (serving size: about 2 turkey cutlets and about 2 tablespoons sauce).

Per serving: CALORIES 263 (11% from fat); FAT 3.3g (saturated fat 0.4g); PROTEIN 42.7g; CARBOHYDRATES 15.6g; FIBER 0.5g; CHOLESTEROL 68mg; IRON 2.5mg; SODIUM 443mg; CALCIUM 12mg

Spinach Salad with Honey-Dijon Vinaigrette

prep: 5 minutes   **POINTS** value: 1

Combine 2 tablespoons white wine vinegar, 1 tablespoon water, 1 tablespoon olive oil, 2 teaspoons honey-Dijon mustard, and ⅛ teaspoon salt in a large bowl. Add 1 (6-ounce) package fresh baby spinach, 1½ cups sliced fresh mushrooms, and 2 tablespoons real bacon bits to bowl; toss gently to coat. Sprinkle with ⅛ teaspoon freshly ground black pepper. **Yield:** 4 servings (serving size: 1¼ cups).

Per serving: CALORIES 90 (45% from fat); FAT 4.5g (saturated fat 1g); PROTEIN 5g; CARBOHYDRATES 10g; FIBER 4g; CHOLESTEROL 3mg; IRON 2.6mg; SODIUM 318mg; CALCIUM 53mg

Salads

POINTS value: 0
Moroccan Mint Limeade | page 111

POINTS value: 1
Toasted Whole Wheat Pita Chips | page 107
Iced Apple Green Tea | page 134

POINTS value: 2
Parmesan Toasts | page 109
Goat Cheese and Lemon Bruschetta | page 136

POINTS value: 3
Pomegranate-Orange Sparkler | page 130

POINTS value: 4
Tuna and White Bean Salad | page 109
**Thai Pork Salad with Lime-Cilantro
    Dressing** | page 131
Tarragon Chicken Salad | page 136

POINTS value: 5
Summer Salmon Salad | page 107
Grilled Steak and Asparagus Salad | page 129
Warm Pork Salad with Apples | page 130
Chicken Caesar Salad | page 133

POINTS value: 6
Shrimp and Orzo Salad | page 110
Fattoush Salad | page 111
Artichoke Rotini Salad with Beans | page 112
Chicken and Bulgur Salad | page 132

POINTS value: 7
Spinach and Tuna Niçoise Salad | page 108
Ginger Chicken with Soba Salad | page 134
Mango and Pecan Chicken Cutlet Salad | page 135

POINTS value: 8
Grilled Salmon and Corn Salad | page 106

Game Plan

1. While grill heats:
- Shuck corn.
- Dice onion, and halve tomatoes.
- Season fish.

2. While fish and corn cook:
- Slice basil, and juice lemon.

3. Toss salmon mixture, and spoon over tomatoes.

Grilled Salmon and Corn Salad

prep: 10 minutes • **cook:** 10 minutes   *POINTS* value: 8

This vibrantly colored summer salad is a snap to prepare when you grill rich salmon and sweet corn on the cob at the same time. Freshly squeezed lemon juice balances and brightens the flavors and adds just the right amount of tartness to this dish.

4	(6-ounce) salmon fillets (about 1 inch thick)
1	teaspoon salt-free lemon pepper seasoning
¼	teaspoon salt
1	ear shucked corn
	Cooking spray
½	cup diced red onion
¼	cup thinly sliced fresh basil
2	tablespoons olive oil
2	tablespoons fresh lemon juice
1	pint cherry tomatoes, halved

1. Prepare grill.

2. Sprinkle skinless sides of salmon fillets with lemon pepper and salt.

3. Place corn and fish, skin sides down, on grill rack coated with cooking spray. Grill, covered, 10 minutes or until corn is lightly charred, turning occasionally, and fish flakes easily when tested with a fork.

4. Remove skin from fish, and cut fish into chunks. Cut corn from cob, and add to fish in a medium bowl. Add onion and next 3 ingredients; toss gently to coat. Serve atop cherry tomato halves. **Yield:** 4 servings (serving size: about 1 cup salmon mixture and ½ cup tomato).

Per serving: CALORIES 350 (43% from fat); FAT 16.9g (saturated fat 2.6g); PROTEIN 40g; CARBOHYDRATES 12g; FIBER 2g; CHOLESTEROL 99mg; IRON 1.4mg; SODIUM 252mg; CALCIUM 26mg

Summer Salmon Salad

prep: 2 minutes • **cook:** 9 minutes   *POINTS* value: 5

Drizzle pan-seared salmon, juicy ripe tomatoes, and crisp cucumbers with a robust and creamy yogurt-based dressing for a light, refreshing supper on a hot day.

   Cooking spray
  3 (6-ounce) salmon fillets (about 1 inch thick)
  ¼ teaspoon salt
  ¼ teaspoon freshly ground black pepper
  ½ cup plain fat-free yogurt
  ½ teaspoon grated lemon rind
  1 tablespoon fresh lemon juice
  1 tablespoon chopped flat-leaf parsley
  1 garlic clove, pressed
  ⅛ teaspoon salt
  1/16 teaspoon freshly ground black pepper
  1 (10-ounce) bag torn Romaine lettuce
  2 large tomatoes, quartered (about 2 cups)
  1 large cucumber, peeled, halved lengthwise, and sliced (about 2 cups)

1. Heat a large nonstick skillet over medium-high heat. Coat pan with cooking spray. Sprinkle skinless sides of salmon fillets with ¼ teaspoon salt and ¼ teaspoon pepper. Add fish to pan; cook 4 minutes on each side or until fish flakes easily when tested with a fork. Remove skin from fish, and break fish into bite-sized pieces.
2. While fish cooks, combine yogurt, grated lemon rind, and next 5 ingredients in a small bowl. Place 1¾ cups lettuce on each of 4 plates. Top each with ½ cup (6 wedges) tomato and ½ cup cucumber. Top salads evenly with fish and drizzle each with 1 tablespoon dressing. **Yield:** 4 servings (serving size: 1 salad).

Per serving: CALORIES 241 (28% from fat); FAT 7.6g (saturated fat 1.2g); PROTEIN 32.9g; CARBOHYDRATES 12.1g; FIBER 3.2g; CHOLESTEROL 75mg; IRON 1.9mg; SODIUM 332mg; CALCIUM 103mg

Toasted Whole Wheat Pita Chips

prep: 4 minutes • **cook:** 6 minutes   *POINTS* value: 1

Preheat oven to 450°. Separate each of 2 (6-inch) whole wheat pitas into 2 rounds; cut each round into 6 wedges. Arrange pita wedges in a single layer on a baking sheet. Coat pita wedges with cooking spray. Combine ½ teaspoon cumin and ¼ teaspoon salt; sprinkle evenly over pita wedges. Bake at 450° for 6 minutes or until lightly browned. **Yield:** 4 servings (serving size: about 6 chips).

Per serving: CALORIES 71 (1% from fat); FAT 0.1g (saturated fat 0g); PROTEIN 3.1g; CARBOHYDRATES 15.6g; FIBER 1.6g; CHOLESTEROL 0mg; IRON 1mg; SODIUM 211mg; CALCIUM 22mg

---

Menu
POINTS value
per serving: 6

Summer Salmon Salad

Toasted Whole Wheat Pita Chips

Game Plan

1. While oven preheats:
- Separate and cut pitas; season pita wedges.
- Season fish.

2. While fish cooks:
- Cook pita wedges.
- Prepare dressing.

3. Quarter tomatoes; peel, halve, and slice cucumbers.

4. Assemble salads.

pictured on page 116

Spinach and Tuna Niçoise Salad

prep: 4 minutes • **cook:** 11 minutes • **other:** 5 minutes   *POINTS* value: 7

Of French origin, niçoise salad is a classic dish made of green beans, tuna, hard-cooked eggs, and herbs. We've simplified the method by using a few convenience items, including packaged ready-to-eat, hard-cooked peeled eggs. Look for them alongside raw eggs in the dairy case of your supermarket. Or if you prefer to boil your own eggs, cook them ahead, cool them, and refrigerate them up to 1 week in their shells.

  1 (12-ounce) package pretrimmed fresh green beans
  4 small red potatoes (about 8 ounces)
  4 precooked peeled eggs (such as Eggland's Best)
  2 (4-ounce) packages lemon and cracked pepper-flavored tuna fillets, drained
  3 tablespoons Dijon mustard
  2 tablespoons extra-virgin olive oil
  2 tablespoons white wine vinegar
  2 tablespoons chopped fresh tarragon
  1 (6-ounce) package fresh baby spinach
16 grape tomatoes
⅓ cup sliced green onions
  2 teaspoons capers

1. Place unopened package of green beans in the center of a microwave-safe platter; arrange potatoes around edges of platter. Microwave green beans according to package directions; remove beans from package, and immediately plunge into a bowl of ice water. Microwave potatoes at HIGH 1 additional minute or until tender. Plunge potatoes into ice water with beans; let stand 5 minutes or until vegetables are cold. Drain. Cut potatoes into quarters.
2. Cut eggs in half lengthwise; remove and reserve 2 egg yolks for another use. Coarsely chop remaining egg yolks and egg whites. Separate fish into large chunks using a fork.
3. Combine mustard and next 3 ingredients in a small bowl, stirring with a whisk.
4. Divide spinach evenly among 4 plates; top spinach evenly with fish, green beans, potatoes, and tomatoes. Sprinkle each salad evenly with green onions, capers, and chopped egg. Drizzle salads evenly with dressing. **Yield:** 4 servings (serving size: 1 salad).

Per serving: CALORIES 364 (27% from fat); FAT 10.8g (saturated fat 1.9g); PROTEIN 27.7g; CARBOHYDRATES 41.1g; FIBER 7.4g; CHOLESTEROL 128mg; IRON 4mg; SODIUM 715mg; CALCIUM 124mg

Tuna and White Bean Salad

prep: 13 minutes   ***POINTS*** value: 4

White balsamic vinegar has a lighter color and flavor than traditional balsamic vinegar. Use white balsamic when additional color is not desired in your dish.

- 2 (6-ounce) cans albacore tuna in water, drained
- 1 (15.5-ounce) can cannellini beans, rinsed and drained
- 2 cups grape tomatoes, halved
- 1 medium chopped peeled cucumber (2 cups)
- ¼ cup thinly sliced red onion
- 4 cups fresh baby spinach
- 2 tablespoons white balsamic vinegar
- 1 tablespoon fresh lemon juice
- 1 tablespoon olive oil
- ½ teaspoon freshly ground black pepper
- ¼ teaspoon salt

1. Combine all ingredients in a large bowl; toss well. **Yield:** 4 servings (serving size: 2½ cups).

Per serving: CALORIES 212 (22% from fat); FAT 5.2g (saturated fat 0.6g); PROTEIN 21.9g; CARBOHYDRATES 21.1g; FIBER 5.8g; CHOLESTEROL 28mg; IRON 3.6mg; SODIUM 578mg; CALCIUM 105mg

Parmesan Toasts

prep: 2 minutes • **cook:** 4 minutes   ***POINTS*** value: 2

Preheat broiler. Place 4 (1-ounce) slices diagonally cut multigrain bread baguette (about 1 inch thick) on a baking sheet. Lightly coat top sides of bread slices with olive oil–flavored cooking spray. Broil 2 minutes or until golden brown. Turn slices over; broil 1 minute. Remove pan from oven, and gently rub top sides of bread slices with ½ of a garlic clove. Sprinkle each slice evenly with ¼ cup grated Parmigiano-Reggiano cheese and ¹⁄₁₆ teaspoon freshly ground black pepper, if desired. Return bread slices to broiler; broil 1 minute or until cheese melts. **Yield:** 4 servings (serving size: 1 toast).

Per serving: CALORIES 99 (22% from fat); FAT 2.4g (saturated fat 1g); PROTEIN 5.4g; CARBOHYDRATES 12.9g; FIBER 0.5g; CHOLESTEROL 5mg; IRON 0.7mg; SODIUM 272mg; CALCIUM 101mg

Menu
POINTS value
per serving: 6

Tuna and White Bean Salad

Parmesan Toasts

Game Plan

1. While broiler preheats:
- Slice bread for toasts.
- Prepare salad.

2. Prepare toasts.

Menu
POINTS value
per serving: 7

Shrimp and Orzo Salad

1 cup cubed melon
POINTS value: 1

Game Plan

1. While water for pasta comes to a boil:
  • Cube melon.

2. While pasta cooks:
  • Chop tomato, green bell pepper, and dill; mince garlic.
  • Measure olives and cheese.
  • Prepare dressing.

3. Toss salad.

Shrimp and Orzo Salad

prep: 4 minutes • **cook:** 16 minutes   *POINTS* value: 6

You'll need to squeeze about 2 to 3 medium lemons to measure ⅓ cup lemon juice for the dressing. To get the most juice from each lemon, be sure your lemons are at room temperature. Before juicing, roll the lemons across the countertop while applying pressure with the palm of your hand.

1¼	cups uncooked orzo (rice-shaped pasta)
¾	pound cooked and peeled medium shrimp
2	cups chopped seeded tomato
1	cup chopped green bell pepper
½	cup sliced ripe olives
⅓	cup fresh lemon juice
2	tablespoons fresh chopped dill
2	tablespoons olive oil
1	teaspoon salt
¼	teaspoon freshly ground black pepper
2	garlic cloves, minced
½	cup (2 ounces) crumbled feta cheese

1. Cook orzo according to package directions, omitting salt and fat; drain. Rinse under cold water until cool; drain.
2. Combine orzo and next 4 ingredients in a large bowl; toss well. Combine lemon juice and next 5 ingredients in a small bowl, stirring with a whisk. Pour lemon juice mixture over orzo mixture; add cheese, and toss gently to coat. Cover and chill until ready to serve. **Yield:** 6 servings (serving size: 1⅓ cups).

Per serving: CALORIES 288 (29% from fat); FAT 9.4g (saturated fat 2.4g); PROTEIN 18.6g; CARBOHYDRATES 32.7g; FIBER 2.9g; CHOLESTEROL 119mg; IRON 2.5mg; SODIUM 727mg; CALCIUM 91mg

Fattoush Salad

prep: 12 minutes • **cook:** 6 minutes   *POINTS* value: 6

Fattoush is a Middle Eastern version of bread salad, made with torn bits of pita and a mixture of chopped vegetables. In this version, we've toasted the pita for extra crunch and added chickpeas to create a complete meal. You'll need to use only ½ cup of the prechopped tricolor bell pepper mix, so plan to use the rest in the Veggie-Egg Scramble on page 19.

  2 (6-inch) whole wheat pitas
Butter-flavored cooking spray
  2 tablespoons white wine vinegar
1½ teaspoons honey
¼ teaspoon ground coriander
  1 tablespoon parsley puree (such as Gourmet Garden)
  1 tablespoon extra-virgin olive oil
  2 medium tomatoes, each cut into 8 wedges
  2 small pickling cucumbers, quartered lengthwise and diced
½ cup prechopped tricolor bell pepper mix
¼ cup prechopped red onion
⅓ cup pitted kalamata olives, halved
  1 (16-ounce) can chickpeas (garbanzo beans), rinsed and drained
½ (10-ounce) package torn romaine lettuce
⅓ cup (1½-ounce) crumbled feta cheese

1. Preheat oven to 450°.
2. Separate each pita into 2 rounds; cut each into 6 wedges. Arrange pita wedges in a single layer on a baking sheet. Coat wedges with cooking spray. Bake at 450° for 6 minutes or until lightly browned.
3. While wedges bake, combine vinegar and next 4 ingredients in a large bowl, stirring with a whisk. Add tomato and remaining 7 ingredients; toss well. Crumble pita wedges and add to salad; toss well. **Yield:** 4 servings (serving size: 2¾ cups).

Per serving: CALORIES 290 (35% from fat); FAT 11.2g (saturated fat 2.8g); PROTEIN 9.6g; CARBOHYDRATES 39.7g; FIBER 7g; CHOLESTEROL 11mg; IRON 4.4mg; SODIUM 659mg; CALCIUM 143mg

Moroccan Mint Limeade

prep: 2 minutes   *POINTS* value: 0

Place 3 cups light limeade (such as Minute Maid), 1 teaspoon ground ginger, 16 fresh mint leaves, and 12 ice cubes in a blender. Process 1 minute or until slushy. **Yield:** 4 servings (serving size: 1 cup).

Per serving: CALORIES 13 (2% from fat); FAT 0g (saturated fat 0g); PROTEIN 0.1g; CARBOHYDRATES 3.4g; FIBER 0.1g; CHOLESTEROL 0mg; IRON 0.1mg; SODIUM 11mg; CALCIUM 1mg

---

Menu
POINTS value
per serving: 6

Fattoush Salad

Moroccan Mint Limeade

Game Plan

1. While oven preheats:
 • Rinse and drain chickpeas.
 • Separate and cut pitas.

2. While pita wedges bake:
 • Prepare dressing.
 • Dice cucumbers, quarter tomatoes, and halve olives.

3. Toss salad.

4. Prepare limeade.

Menu

POINTS value
per serving: 7

**Artichoke Rotini Salad
with Beans**

**1 cup mixed
strawberry and kiwi slices**
POINTS value: 1

Game Plan

1. While water for pasta comes to
a boil:
  • Rinse and drain artichokes and
  beans.

2. While pasta cooks:
  • Halve tomatoes, mince garlic,
  and chop oregano.

3. Toss salad.

Artichoke Rotini Salad with Beans

prep: 5 minutes • **cook:** 15 minutes

POINTS value: 6

Multigrain pasta boasts almost twice the fiber of traditional pasta, plus it has more protein. Both of these factors help you feel fuller for a longer period after eating.

1 cup uncooked multigrain rotini
1 (15-ounce) can black beans, rinsed and drained
1 (14-ounce) can quartered artichoke hearts, rinsed and drained
1 cup grape tomatoes, cut in half
1 cup prechopped green bell pepper
2 garlic cloves, minced
3 tablespoons cider vinegar
3 tablespoons extra-virgin olive oil
1 tablespoon chopped fresh oregano
½ teaspoon salt

1. Cook pasta according to package directions, omitting salt and fat. Drain.
2. Combine beans and remaining ingredients in a large bowl; add pasta, and toss gently to coat. **Yield:** 4 servings (serving size: about 1⅔ cups).

Per serving: CALORIES 275 (39% from fat); FAT 11.9g (saturated fat 1.5g); PROTEIN 9.6g; CARBOHYDRATES 38.5g; FIBER 7.9g; CHOLESTEROL 0mg; IRON 3mg; SODIUM 613mg; CALCIUM 48mg

Balsamic Chicken and Mushrooms | page 95

Chicken with Peanut Sauce and
Lo Mein Noodles | page 98

Mango and Pecan Chicken Cutlet Salad | page 135

Spinach and Tuna Niçoise Salad | page 108

Grilled Steak and Asparagus
Salad | page 129

**Shrimp Salad Lettuce
Wraps** | page 138

118

Asian-Style Turkey Burgers | page 152

Grilled Open-Faced Mediterranean Sandwiches | page 142

Chicken and Rice Soup with
Greens | page 161

Quick Italian Chicken Soup | page 160

Chili Picante | page 157

Fresh Pineapple-Lime
Dessert Salsa | page 185

Double-Chocolate
Pudding | page 171

Broiled Berries and Peaches with Ice Cream | page 177

Spicy Chocolate Soup | page 164

Strawberry
Ice Cream Sundaes | page 188

pictured on page 117

Grilled Steak and Asparagus Salad

prep: 5 minutes • **cook:** 8 minutes • **other:** 5 minutes   *POINTS* value: 5

Nothing says spring like this warm, grilled salad with savory steak and asparagus. This dish is best served with bread to soak up the delicious dressing.

1   (1-pound) flank steak
4   (¼-inch-thick) slices red onion
1   pound asparagus spears, trimmed
Cooking spray
1   tablespoon red wine vinegar
2   tablespoons Dijon mustard
1   tablespoon extra-virgin olive oil
¼   teaspoon salt
⅛   teaspoon freshly ground black pepper

1. Prepare grill.

2. Coat both sides of flank steak, onion, and asparagus with cooking spray. Place meat and vegetables on a grill rack coated with cooking spray; grill 4 to 5 minutes on each side or to desired degree of doneness. Remove from grill; let stand 5 minutes.

3. Combine vinegar and remaining 4 ingredients in a large bowl, stirring with a whisk.

4. Slice onion rings and asparagus in half, and cut steak diagonally across grain into thin slices. Add steak and vegetables to dressing; toss gently to coat. **Yield:** 4 servings (serving size: 1¼ cups).

Per serving: CALORIES 237 (38% from fat); FAT 10g (saturated fat 2.9g); PROTEIN 27.4g; CARBOHYDRATES 9.4g; FIBER 2.8g; CHOLESTEROL 37mg; IRON 2.8mg; SODIUM 404mg; CALCIUM 61mg

Menu
POINTS value
per serving: 7

Grilled Steak and Asparagus Salad

1 (1-ounce) slice French bread, grilled
POINTS value: 2

Game Plan

1. While grill heats:
  • Trim asparagus, and slice onion.
  • Slice French bread.

2. While steak and vegetables cook:
  • Prepare dressing.

3. While steak stands, cook bread.

4. Toss salad.

Game Plan

1. Season pork.

2. While pork cooks:
  • Prepare dressing.
  • Core and slice apple.

3. Prepare sparkler.

4. Toss and assemble salads.

Warm Pork Salad with Apples

prep: 6 minutes • **cook:** 7 minutes

POINTS value: 5

Pork and apples are simply meant for each other. The pungent dressing marries well with tart Granny Smith apples.

    6 teaspoons olive oil, divided
    1 (1-pound) pork tenderloin, cut into 12 slices
 1¼ teaspoons ground cumin, divided
   ½ teaspoon salt, divided
   ¼ teaspoon black pepper, divided
    2 tablespoons cider vinegar
    2 teaspoons light brown sugar
    1 (7-ounce) package torn radicchio and butter lettuce (such as Fresh Express Riviera)
    1 large Granny Smith apple, cored and thinly sliced

1. Heat 2 teaspoons of oil in a large nonstick skillet over medium-high heat. Sprinkle pork evenly with 1 teaspoon cumin, ¼ teaspoon salt, and ⅛ teaspoon pepper. Add pork to pan; cook 3 minutes on each side or until done.
2. Combine vinegar, brown sugar, remaining 4 teaspoons oil, remaining ¼ teaspoon cumin, remaining ¼ teaspoon salt, and remaining ⅛ teaspoon pepper in a small bowl, stirring with a whisk.
3. Place lettuce, apple, and 2 tablespoons dressing in a large bowl; toss gently to coat. Divide salad evenly among 4 plates; top each with 3 slices of pork, and drizzle remaining dressing evenly over pork. **Yield:** 4 servings (serving size: 3 slices pork, 2 cups salad, and 1 teaspoon dressing).

Per serving: CALORIES 237 (42% from fat); FAT 11g (saturated fat 2.3g); PROTEIN 23.4g; CARBOHYDRATES 12g; FIBER 2.1g; CHOLESTEROL 63mg; IRON 1.6mg; SODIUM 344mg; CALCIUM 16mg

Pomegranate-Orange Sparkler

prep: 2 minutes

POINTS value: 3

Combine 1 cup chilled pomegranate juice, 1 cup chilled orange juice, and ¼ cup sugar in a large pitcher; stir until sugar dissolves. Stir in 2 cups chilled sparkling water and serve immediately over ice with lime wedges. **Yield:** 4 servings (serving size: 1 cup sparkler and 1 lime wedge).

Per serving: CALORIES 154 (1% from fat); FAT 0.2g (saturated fat 0g); PROTEIN 0.8g; CARBOHYDRATES 38.7g; FIBER 0.1g; CHOLESTEROL 0mg; IRON 0.2mg; SODIUM 13mg; CALCIUM 18mg

Thai Pork Salad with Lime-Cilantro Dressing

prep: 12 minutes • **cook:** 7 minutes   *POINTS* value: 4

If you can only find a package that contains 2 (1-pound) pork tenderloins, wrap the extra piece of pork in plastic wrap and foil, and freeze. Try using it in the Jerk-Seasoned Pork Tenderloin on page 88.

1	pound pork tenderloin, cut into 4 pieces
¼	teaspoon salt
⅛	teaspoon black pepper
	Cooking spray
1½	ounces uncooked cellophane noodles
2	cups coleslaw
2	cups shredded iceberg lettuce
1	large cucumber, peeled, halved, and thinly sliced (2¼ cups)
½	cup thinly sliced red onion
⅓	cup fresh lime juice
2	tablespoons chopped fresh cilantro
4	teaspoons sugar
4	teaspoons fish sauce

1. Prepare grill.

2. Place pork pieces between 2 sheets of heavy-duty plastic wrap; pound each piece to ½-inch thickness with a meat mallet or small heavy skillet. Sprinkle evenly with salt and pepper.

3. Place pork on a grill rack coated with cooking spray; grill 4 to 5 minutes on each side or until done. Cut each piece into thin slices. Set aside and keep warm.

4. While pork cooks, cook noodles according to package directions, omitting salt and fat; drain and rinse under cold water. Coarsely chop noodles and place in a large bowl. Stir in coleslaw, and next 3 ingredients.

5. Combine lime juice and remaining 3 ingredients in a small bowl, stirring with a whisk; reserve 3 tablespoons dressing. Pour remaining dressing over noodle mixture; toss gently to coat. Divide salad evenly among 4 bowls; top each with pork slices and drizzle evenly with reserved 3 tablespoons lime juice mixture.

Yield: 4 servings (serving size: 3 ounces pork and 1¾ cups salad).

Per serving: CALORIES 217 (17% from fat); FAT 4.1g (saturated fat 1.4g); PROTEIN 24.2g; CARBOHYDRATES 20.7g; FIBER 2g; CHOLESTEROL 63mg; IRON 1.7mg; SODIUM 582mg; CALCIUM 40mg

Menu
POINTS value
per serving: 5

Thai Pork Salad with Lime-Cilantro Dressing

1 large orange
POINTS value: 1

Game Plan

1. While grill heats:
- Bring water for noodles to a boil.
- Measure coleslaw and lettuce.
- Slice onion; chop cilantro.
- Peel, halve, and slice cucumber.
- Pound pork.

2. While pork cooks:
- Cook noodles.
- Prepare dressing.

3. Toss and assemble salads.

Menu
POINTS value
per serving: 7

Chicken and Bulgur Salad

1 (6-inch) whole wheat pita,
quartered and warmed
POINTS value: 1

Game Plan

1. While water for bulgur comes to
a boil:
- Chop chicken, cucumber, and
parsley; halve tomatoes.

2. While bulgur cooks:
- Prepare dressing.

3. Rinse and drain bulgur; toss
salad.

Chicken and Bulgur Salad

prep: 4 minutes • **cook:** 16 minutes   **POINTS** value: 6

**Bulgur—wheat berries that have been steamed, dried, and ground—is
a smart choice if you want to incorporate more fiber into your diet.
Adding cold water to the bulgur right in the pan and rinsing it in
a sieve under cold running water eliminates the need to chill this
recipe before serving. This salad keeps for several days in the fridge
and makes a great brown-bag lunch.**

2	cups water
1	cup quick-cooking bulgur
1	teaspoon grated lemon rind
3	tablespoons fresh lemon juice
1	small garlic clove, pressed
¼	teaspoon salt
⅛	teaspoon freshly ground black pepper
1	tablespoon olive oil
2	cups chopped cooked chicken breast
1	cup grape tomatoes, halved
1	cup chopped English cucumber (about ⅓ medium)
¼	cup chopped fresh flat-leaf parsley

1. Place water in a medium saucepan; bring to a boil. Stir in bulgur; cover, reduce
heat to medium, and simmer 12 minutes.
2. While bulgur cooks, combine lemon rind and next 5 ingredients in a large bowl;
stir with a whisk.
3. Add cold water to pan to cool bulgur. Pour water and bulgur into a sieve; rinse
with cold water. Drain well, pressing bulgur with the back of a spoon to remove
as much water as possible.
4. Add bulgur to dressing; toss gently to coat. Add chicken, tomato, and remaining
ingredients; toss well. Serve immediately, or cover and chill. **Yield:** 4 servings (serving size: 1 cup).

Per serving: CALORIES 302 (20% from fat); FAT 6.7g (saturated fat 1.2g); PROTEIN 27.4g; CARBOHYDRATES 33.7g; FIBER 7.9g; CHOLESTEROL 60mg;
IRON 2.2mg; SODIUM 207mg; CALCIUM 47mg

Chicken Caesar Salad

prep: 8 minutes   *POINTS* value: 5

Tangy dressing, crunchy croutons, and a characteristic Mediterranean bite make Caesar salad hard to turn down. Our lightened version has all of the zing of the original but uses lemon juice for the dressing's base instead of egg yolks and heavy oil. Although rotisserie chicken breast or leftover cooked chicken will work for this recipe, grilled chicken makes a delicious variation.

¼   cup lemon juice
1   tablespoon olive oil
2   teaspoons Dijon mustard
1½   teaspoons red wine vinegar
1   teaspoon Worcestershire sauce
2   garlic cloves, minced
1   tablespoon capers
6   cups chopped romaine lettuce
2   cups chopped cooked chicken breast
2   tablespoons shredded fresh Parmesan cheese
1   cup fat-free croutons

1. Combine lemon juice and next 6 ingredients in a small bowl; stir with a whisk.
2. Combine lettuce, chicken, cheese, and croutons in a large bowl; pour dressing over salad. Toss gently to coat. **Yield:** 4 servings (serving size: 2¼ cups).

Per serving: CALORIES 214 (31% from fat); FAT 7.3g (saturated fat 1.8g); PROTEIN 25.1g; CARBOHYDRATES 10.6g; FIBER 1.9g; CHOLESTEROL 62mg; IRON 1.7mg; SODIUM 332mg; CALCIUM 82mg

Menu
POINTS value
per serving: 7

Chicken Caesar Salad

1 (1-ounce) slice toasted ciabatta
POINTS value: 2

Game Plan

1. While oven preheats:
- Slice ciabatta, and arrange on baking sheet.
- Prepare dressing.

2. While ciabatta toasts:
- Toss salad.

Menu
POINTS value
per serving: 8

Ginger Chicken with Soba Salad

Iced Apple Green Tea

Game Plan

1. While water for noodles comes to a boil:
   - Mince ginger, shred carrot, grate cucumber, and chop cilantro.

2. While noodles cook:
   - Cook chicken.
   - Prepare dressing.
   - Prepare tea.

3. While tea brews:
   - Toss noodles, and assemble salads.

Ginger Chicken with Soba Salad

prep: 2 minutes • **cook:** 18 minutes   *POINTS* value: 7

Grated carrot and fresh cilantro give this hearty noodle salad an extra dimension of tantalizing taste and color. Look for soba noodles, often labeled as buckwheat noodles, in the ethnic-food section of your supermarket.

4	ounces soba noodles
3	teaspoons canola oil, divided
4	(6-ounce) boneless, skinless chicken breast halves
3	tablespoons minced fresh ginger, divided
¼	teaspoon salt
3	tablespoons reduced-sodium soy sauce
2	tablespoons rice vinegar
2	green onions, thinly sliced
¾	cup shredded carrot
½	cup grated cucumber
¼	cup chopped fresh cilantro

1. Cook noodles according to package directions, omitting salt and fat. Drain; rinse with cold water.
2. While noodles cook, heat 2 teaspoons oil in a large nonstick skillet over medium heat. Sprinkle chicken with 2 tablespoons ginger and ¼ teaspoon salt. Cook 7 to 8 minutes on each side or until done. Set aside and keep warm.
3. Combine soy sauce, vinegar, remaining 1 tablespoon ginger, and remaining 1 teaspoon oil in a large bowl, stirring with a whisk. Add noodles, onions, carrot, and cucumber; toss well. Divide noodle mixture evenly among 4 plates. Thinly slice each chicken breast; arrange evenly on top of noodles. Sprinkle with cilantro.
Yield: 4 servings (serving size: 1 chicken breast and ¾ cup salad).

Per serving: CALORIES 344 (16% from fat); FAT 6.3g (saturated fat 0.8g); PROTEIN 43.6g; CARBOHYDRATES 26.8g; FIBER 2.7g; CHOLESTEROL 99mg; IRON 2.3mg; SODIUM 676mg; CALCIUM 50mg

Iced Apple Green Tea

prep: 2 minutes • **cook:** 3 minutes • **other:** 5 minutes   *POINTS* value: 1

Bring 1 cup water and 1 tablespoon "measures like sugar" calorie-free sweetener (such as Splenda) to a boil in a small saucepan. Remove from heat and add 4 green tea bags to pan; let stand 5 minutes. Remove and discard tea bags. Combine 1 cup water, 2 cups apple juice, and brewed tea in a pitcher. Pour evenly into 4 glasses. Serve with lemon slices. **Yield:** 4 cups (serving size: 1 cup tea and 1 lemon slice).

Per serving: CALORIES 57 (0% from fat); FAT 0g (saturated fat 0g); PROTEIN 0.1g; CARBOHYDRATES 14.5g; FIBER 0g; CHOLESTEROL 0mg; IRON 0mg; SODIUM 14mg; CALCIUM 0mg

pictured on page 115

Mango and Pecan Chicken Cutlet Salad

prep: 5 minutes • **cook:** 7 minutes   *POINTS* value: 7

A generous portion of lightly breaded chicken slices is tossed with tender baby lettuces and coated with a citrusy vinaigrette in this main-dish salad. If you cannot find fresh mangoes, substitute refrigerated jarred mangoes.

- 1 pound chicken cutlets (about 5 cutlets)
- ¼ teaspoon salt
- ⅛ teaspoon black pepper
- 3 egg whites
- ¾ cup Italian-seasoned breadcrumbs
- 2 teaspoons olive oil
- Olive oil–flavored cooking spray
- 1 (5-ounce) package sweet baby greens (such as Fresh Express)
- 1 cup chopped mango (1 large)
- 2 tablespoons chopped pecans, toasted
- ¼ cup reduced-fat olive oil vinaigrette
- 4 teaspoons fresh lime juice

1. Sprinkle chicken evenly with salt and pepper. Dip chicken in egg whites; dredge in breadcrumbs.
2. Heat oil in a large nonstick skillet coated with cooking spray over medium-high heat. Add chicken to pan; cook 3 minutes on each side or until done. Slice chicken into thin strips; set aside and keep warm.
3. Place greens, mango, pecans, and chicken in a large bowl. Drizzle with vinaigrette and lime juice; toss gently to coat. **Yield:** 4 servings (serving size: 1¼ cups).

Per serving: CALORIES 312 (30% from fat); FAT 10.4g (saturated fat 1.4g); PROTEIN 31.6g; CARBOHYDRATES 23.2; FIBER 2.3g; CHOLESTEROL 66mg; IRON 2.6mg; SODIUM 577mg; CALCIUM 67mg

Menu
POINTS value
per serving: 9

Mango and Pecan Chicken Cutlet Salad

2 sesame flatbread crackers
POINTS value: 2

Game Plan

1. Season and dredge chicken.

2. While chicken cooks:
  • Chop mango.
  • Toast pecans.
  • Juice lime.

3. Toss salad.

Menu
POINTS value
per serving: 6

Tarragon Chicken Salad

Goat Cheese and Lemon Bruschetta

Game Plan

1. While oven preheats:
- Cut baguette into slices.
- Prepare goat cheese mixture.
- Chop tarragon.
- Season chicken.

2. While chicken cooks:
- Toast baguette slices.
- Prepare dressing.
- Slice fennel and onion.

3. Toss salad, and spread goat cheese mixture onto baguette slices.

Tarragon Chicken Salad

prep: 12 minutes • **cook:** 7 minutes   *POINTS* value: 4

Fennel adds a refreshing, pleasant note that complements the tarragon-tinged chicken. Look for small, heavy white fennel bulbs that are firm and free of cracks or browning.

1	pound chicken cutlets (about 5 cutlets)
1	tablespoon plus 2 teaspoons chopped fresh tarragon, divided
¾	teaspoon salt, divided
¼	teaspoon freshly ground black pepper, divided
5	teaspoons olive oil, divided
1	tablespoon fresh lemon juice
5	cups torn romaine lettuce
1½	cups thinly sliced fennel bulb (about 1 medium bulb)
½	cup thinly sliced red onion

1. Sprinkle chicken with 1 tablespoon tarragon, ½ teaspoon salt, and ⅛ teaspoon pepper. Heat 2 teaspoons oil in a large nonstick skillet over medium-high heat; add chicken to pan. Cook 3 minutes on each side or until done.
2. While chicken cooks, combine remaining 3 teaspoons oil, lemon juice, remaining 2 teaspoons tarragon, remaining ¼ teaspoon salt, and remaining ⅛ teaspoon pepper in a large bowl; stir with a whisk. Add lettuce, fennel, and red onion. Cut chicken into slices; add to salad. Toss well. **Yield:** 4 servings (serving size: 2¼ cups).

Per serving: CALORIES 214 (32% from fat); FAT 7.6g (saturated fat 1.2g); PROTEIN 28.1g; CARBOHYDRATES 8.6g; FIBER 3.6g; CHOLESTEROL 66mg; IRON 2mg; SODIUM 547mg; CALCIUM 73mg

Goat Cheese and Lemon Bruschetta

prep: 4 minutes • **cook:** 7 minutes   *POINTS* value: 2

Preheat oven to 350°. Toast 8 (½-inch-thick) slices whole wheat bread baguette at 350° for 7 minutes or until lightly browned. While bread toasts, combine ½ cup (2 ounces) crumbled goat cheese and 1 teaspoon grated lemon rind in a small bowl. Spread about 1 tablespoon goat cheese mixture over each toasted baguette slice. **Yield:** 4 servings (serving size: 2 baguette slices).

Per serving: CALORIES 82 (47% from fat); FAT 4.3g (saturated fat 2.9g); PROTEIN 4.1g; CARBOHYDRATES 6.2g; FIBER 0.3g; CHOLESTEROL 11mg; IRON 0.5mg; SODIUM 139mg; CALCIUM 43mg

Sandwiches

pictured on page 118

Shrimp Salad Lettuce Wraps

prep: 15 minutes

POINTS value: 5

Menu
POINTS value
per serving: 5

Shrimp Salad Lettuce Wraps

1 cup red bell pepper strips
and carrot sticks
POINTS value: 0

Game Plan

1. Slice green onions; cut cucumber and radishes into matchstick-cut slices.

2. Prepare shrimp mixture.

3. Assemble wraps.

4. Cut red bell peppers into strips and carrots into sticks.

Lettuce leaves cradle this light and creamy shrimp salad. To make these wraps ahead, prepare the shrimp mixture, lettuce leaves, cucumbers, and radishes, and store them in separate containers in the refrigerator. Assemble the wraps just before serving.

⅓   cup thinly sliced green onions
¼   cup (2-ounces) tub light cream cheese, softened
¼   cup light mayonnaise
¼   cup plain fat-free yogurt
½   teaspoon garlic powder
¼   teaspoon dried dill
¼   teaspoon salt
¼   teaspoon black pepper
1   pound cooked peeled medium shrimp, chopped
8   large Bibb lettuce leaves
1   cup matchstick-cut cucumber
½   cup matchstick-cut radishes

1. Combine first 8 ingredients in a medium bowl; stir in shrimp.

2. Spoon about ⅓ cup shrimp mixture down center of each lettuce leaf. Top each wrap evenly with cucumber and radishes. **Yield:** 4 servings (serving size: 2 lettuce wraps).

Per serving: CALORIES 212 (36% from fat); FAT 8.5g (saturated fat 2.7g); PROTEIN 26.6g; CARBOHYDRATES 5.8g; FIBER 0.9g; CHOLESTEROL 233mg; IRON 4.2mg; SODIUM 598mg; CALCIUM 104mg

Open-Faced Egg Salad on Multigrain Toast

prep: 8 minutes • **cook:** 2 minutes   *POINTS* value: 5

Using precooked eggs from the dairy section of your supermarket makes this savory egg salad sandwich a snap to prepare. To cook your own eggs, place the eggs in a single layer in a saucepan with enough cool water to cover the eggs by at least 1 inch. Cover the pan, and bring just to a boil; immediately turn off the heat. Let the eggs stand, covered, for 15 minutes. Run the eggs under cold water until completely cooled before you peel them.

8	peeled hard-cooked eggs (such as Eggland's Best)
¼	cup light mayonnaise
¼	cup plain fat-free yogurt
¼	cup minced celery
1	tablespoon grated fresh onion
½	teaspoon salt
½	teaspoon Dijon mustard
¼	teaspoon freshly ground black pepper
4	teaspoons light mayonnaise
4	(1-ounce) slices multigrain bread, toasted
4	tomato slices
1	tablespoon thinly sliced fresh basil

1. Cut eggs in half lengthwise; remove yolks. Discard 4 whole yolks. Combine remaining yolks, ¼ cup mayonnaise, and yogurt in a medium bowl; stir until smooth. Coarsely chop egg whites; add to yolk mixture. Stir in celery and next 4 ingredients.

2. Spread 1 teaspoon mayonnaise over 1 side of each slice of toast. Top each with 1 tomato slice and ½ cup egg mixture. Sprinkle each evenly with basil.

Yield: 4 servings (serving size: 1 sandwich).

Per serving: CALORIES 243 (47% from fat); FAT 12.8g (saturated fat 2.6g); PROTEIN 13.7g; CARBOHYDRATES 18.6g; FIBER 2.2g; CHOLESTEROL 219mg; IRON 1.6mg; SODIUM 701mg; CALCIUM 140mg

Menu
POINTS value
per serving: 6

Open-Faced Egg Salad on Multigrain Toast

1 cup red seedless grapes
POINTS value: 1

Game Plan

1. Mince celery, and grate onion.

2. While bread toasts:
- Prepare egg mixture.
- Slice tomato and basil.
- Rinse and drain grapes.

3. Assemble sandwiches.

Menu

POINTS value
per serving: 7

Black Bean Burgers

1 ounce baked tortilla chips
(12 to 14 chips)
POINTS value: 2

Game Plan

1. Chop cilantro and green onions;
mince garlic.

2. Cook patties.

3. Assemble burgers.

Black Bean Burgers

prep: 10 minutes • **cook:** 5 minutes   *POINTS* value: 5

Accompany these high-fiber, Southwestern-flavored burgers with baked tortilla chips. The bean mixture may seem a little sticky, but the patties bind together nicely once they begin to cook.

  1   (15-ounce) can black beans, rinsed and drained
  ⅓   cup dry breadcrumbs
  2   tablespoons chopped fresh cilantro
  ¼   cup chopped green onions
  1   garlic clove, minced
  1   large egg
  ½   teaspoon chili powder
  ½   teaspoon ground cumin
  ⅛   teaspoon salt
  2   teaspoons canola oil
  4   (1.5-ounce) white-wheat hamburger buns (such as Nature's Own)
  4   green leaf lettuce leaves
  ½   cup refrigerated fresh salsa

1. Place beans in a large bowl; partially mash with a potato masher. Stir in breadcrumbs and next 7 ingredients. Divide bean mixture into 4 equal portions, shaping each into a ½-inch-thick patty.
2. Heat oil in a large nonstick skillet over medium-high heat. Add patties to pan; cook 2 to 3 minutes on each side or until patties are browned.
3. Place 1 patty on bottom half of each of 4 buns. Top with 1 lettuce leaf, 2 tablespoons salsa, and top half of each bun. **Yield:** 4 servings (serving size: 1 burger).

Per serving: CALORIES 248 (23% from fat); FAT 6.5g (saturated fat 1.2g); PROTEIN 12.2g; CARBOHYDRATES 41.4g; FIBER 9.9g; CHOLESTEROL 53mg; IRON 4.7mg; SODIUM 740mg; CALCIUM 313mg

Vegetable Wraps with Hummus and Feta

prep: 18 minutes   *POINTS* value: 8

The soft, tender Mediterranean flatbread offers a delightful contrast in texture to the crisp vegetable filling in this hearty meatless wrap. Look for the flatbread on the bread aisle or in the deli section of your supermarket.

1	medium cucumber, peeled and chopped
1	cup grape tomatoes, halved
½	cup chopped red onion
¼	cup chopped bottled roasted red bell peppers
1½	tablespoons chopped pitted kalamata olives
1½	tablespoons chopped fresh dill
1	tablespoon grated lemon rind
2	(2.8-ounce) Mediterranean flatbreads (such as Toufayan)
¼	cup hummus
2	Romaine lettuce leaves
1½	tablespoons crumbled feta cheese

1. Combine first 7 ingredients in a medium bowl; toss well.

2. Spread 2 tablespoons hummus onto each flatbread; top with 1 lettuce leaf. Spoon vegetable mixture evenly onto half of each flatbread, leaving a ½-inch border around edges. Top evenly with feta; fold flatbread in half over vegetable mixture.

Yield: 2 servings (serving size: 1 wrap).

Per serving: CALORIES 397 (33% from fat); FAT 14.5g (saturated fat 3.2g); PROTEIN 13.2g; CARBOHYDRATES 54.1g; FIBER 7.4g; CHOLESTEROL 6mg; IRON 2mg; SODIUM 744mg; CALCIUM 83mg

Menu
POINTS value
per serving: 8

Vegetable Wraps with Hummus and Feta

1 cup mixed greens with fat-free balsamic dressing
POINTS value: 0

Game Plan

1. Measure and prepare vegetables.

2. Assemble wraps.

3. Toss salad.

pictured on page 120

Grilled Open-Faced Mediterranean Sandwiches

prep: 6 minutes • **cook:** 9 minutes   *POINTS* value: 5

Grilled romaine hearts are the perfect partners for these open-faced sandwiches. Be sure to keep the core of the hearts intact to hold the leaves together while cooking. Use dense bread, such as sourdough, for the sandwich so that it will be firm enough for grilling.

1   (1-pound) eggplant, cut into ¼-inch slices
3   tablespoons light Caesar dressing, divided
Cooking spray
4   (1.5-ounce) slices sourdough bread
4   (1-ounce) slices part-skim mozzarella cheese
8   thin slices tomato
¼   teaspoon salt
¼   teaspoon freshly ground black pepper

1. Prepare grill.
2. Brush eggplant slices evenly with 1½ tablespoons dressing. Place eggplant slices on grill rack coated with cooking spray; grill 3 to 4 minutes on each side or until tender, brushing occasionally with remaining dressing. Remove from grill.
3. Top each of 4 bread slices with 1 slice eggplant, 1 slice cheese, and 2 slices tomato. Sprinkle salt and pepper over sandwiches. Place sandwiches, bread side down, on grill rack. Grill 3 minutes or until bread is toasted and cheese melts. Serve immediately. **Yield:** 4 servings (serving size: 1 sandwich).

Per serving: CALORIES 254 (26% from fat); FAT 7.2g (saturated fat 4g); PROTEIN 14g; CARBOHYDRATES 34.9g; FIBER 4.1g; CHOLESTEROL 16mg; IRON 2mg; SODIUM 697mg; CALCIUM 240mg

Grilled Romaine Salad

prep: 5 minutes • **cook:** 5 minutes   *POINTS* value: 1

Cut 2 romaine hearts in half lengthwise; coat with olive oil-flavored cooking spray. Place romaine hearts, cut sides down, on grill rack coated with cooking spray. Grill 5 minutes or until tender and browned. Transfer to a serving plate. Drizzle evenly with 2 tablespoons light Caesar dressing and sprinkle evenly with ¼ cup shaved Parmesan cheese. Serve immediately. **Yield:** 4 servings (serving size: ½ romaine heart).

Per serving: CALORIES 52 (36% from fat); FAT 2.1g (saturated fat 1.1g); PROTEIN 3.5g; CARBOHYDRATES 5.3g; FIBER 1.4g; CHOLESTEROL 5mg; IRON 1.3mg; SODIUM 194mg; CALCIUM 126mg

---

Menu
POINTS value
per serving: 6

Grilled Open-Faced
Mediterranean Sandwiches

Grilled Romaine Salad

Game Plan

1. While grill heats:
  • Slice eggplant and tomato; halve romaine hearts.
  • Shave Parmesan cheese.

2. Grill eggplant and romaine hearts.

3. Assemble sandwiches.

4. While sandwiches grill:
  • Drizzle romaine hearts with dressing, and top with cheese.

Grilled Portobello Sandwiches

prep: 3 minutes • **cook:** 8 minutes   ***POINTS*** value: 5

Serve the leftover Roasted Red Pepper Sauce (see recipe below) with baked tortilla chips. One tablespoon has a *POINTS* value of 0. If you don't have an indoor electric grill, use a large nonstick skillet or a grill pan heated over medium heat. Place the sandwiches in the pan, and top with a cast-iron skillet; press gently to flatten. Cook for 2 minutes on each side or until both sides of the buns are golden brown.

- 4   (4-inch) Portobello mushrooms caps
- 2   tablespoons balsamic vinegar
- 1   teaspoon extravirgin olive oil
- ¼   teaspoon garlic salt
- Cooking spray
- ½   cup (4 ounces) goat cheese
- 4   (1.5-ounce) white-wheat hamburger buns (such as Nature's Own)
- 1   cup arugula leaves
- ¼   cup Roasted Red Pepper Sauce (see recipe below)

1. Preheat indoor electric grill.
2. Remove brown gills from the undersides of portobello mushrooms using a spoon; discard gills. Combine vinegar, oil, and garlic salt in a small bowl, stirring with a whisk. Brush mushroom caps with vinegar mixture.
3. Heat a large nonstick skillet over medium-high heat. Coat with cooking spray. Cook mushrooms 3 minutes on each side or until tender.
4. Spread goat cheese evenly on cut sides of buns. Place mushrooms on bottom halves of buns. Cover with top halves. Coat tops and bottoms of buns with cooking spray. Cook sandwiches in panini press or electric grill 1 minute or until tops and bottoms are golden brown.
5. Remove top of each sandwich; add arugula and 1 tablespoon Roasted Red Pepper Sauce, and recover with tops of buns. **Yield:** 4 servings (serving size: 1 sandwich).

Per serving: CALORIES 232 (37% from fat); FAT 9.5g (saturated fat 4.8g); PROTEIN 13g; CARBOHYDRATES 29.4g; FIBER 6.7g; CHOLESTEROL 13mg; IRON 4.1mg; SODIUM 485mg; CALCIUM 330mg

Sweet Potato Fries with Roasted Red Pepper Sauce

prep: 2 minutes • **cook:** 18 minutes   ***POINTS*** value: 1

Preheat oven, and bake 3 cups frozen sweet potato fries according to package directions. Place 1 (12-ounce) jar roasted red bell peppers, ⅓ cup ketchup, and 2 teaspoons smoked paprika (such as McCormick) in a blender; process until smooth. Serve ½ cup with fries and ¼ cup with Grilled Portobello Sandwiches (see recipe above). Store remaining sauce in an airtight container in the refrigerator for up to 1 week. **Yield:** 4 servings (serving size: ¾ cup fries and 2 tablespoons sauce).

Per serving: CALORIES 80 (1% from fat); FAT 0.1g (saturated fat 0g); PROTEIN 1g; CARBOHYDRATES 17.9g; FIBER 2.4g; CHOLESTEROL 0mg; IRON 0.4mg; SODIUM 170mg; CALCIUM 17mg

---

Menu
POINTS value
per serving: 6

Grilled Portobello Sandwiches

Sweet Potato Fries with Roasted Red Pepper Sauce

Game Plan

1. While oven and indoor electric grill preheat:
- Remove gills from portobellos.
- Prepare vinegar mixture.

2. While fries cook:
- Prepare red pepper sauce.
- Cook mushrooms, and prepare sandwiches.

Menu
***POINTS* value**
per serving: 8

Roast Beef Panini Sandwiches with Goat Cheese–Horseradish Spread

1 cup mixed cucumber slices, cherry tomatoes, and celery sticks
***POINTS* value: 0**

Game Plan

1. While panini press or indoor electric grill preheats:
  • Slice red onion and cucumber; cut celery into sticks.

2. While onion cooks:
  • Prepare goat cheese mixture.
  • Spread goat cheese mixture and mustard on baguette.

3. Assemble and cook sandwiches.

Roast Beef Panini Sandwiches with Goat Cheese–Horseradish Spread

prep: 7 minutes • **cook:** 7 minutes   ***POINTS* value: 8**

The creamy and spicy spread transforms these simple roast beef sandwiches into something extraordinary. To prepare the sandwiches quickly, combine the ingredients for the spread, and begin assembling the sandwiches while the onions cook.

  1   small red onion, thinly sliced
Cooking spray
  2   ounces goat cheese, softened
  2   tablespoons light mayonnaise
  2   tablespoons prepared horseradish
  2   tablespoons spicy brown mustard
  1   (8.5-ounce) whole wheat baguette, halved lengthwise
  ⅔   pound thinly sliced low-sodium deli roast beef (such as Boar's Head)
  2   cups arugula leaves

1. Preheat panini press or indoor electric grill.
2. Coat red onion slices with cooking spray. Cook in panini press or indoor electric grill 4 to 5 minutes or until tender; remove from grill.
3. While onion cooks, combine goat cheese, and next 2 ingredients in small bowl; stir until well blended.
4. Spread goat cheese mixture on top half of baguette. Spread mustard on bottom half of baguette; layer evenly with roast beef, grilled onion, and arugula. Replace top half of baguette. Cut baguette into 4 sandwiches. Cook sandwiches in panini press or in indoor electric grill 3 to 4 minutes or until golden brown. **Yield:** 4 servings (serving size: 1 sandwich).

Per serving: CALORIES 352 (28% from fat); FAT 11g (saturated fat 4.8g); PROTEIN 29.5g; CARBOHYDRATES 31.7g; FIBER 2.1g; CHOLESTEROL 54mg; IRON 4.2mg; SODIUM 661mg; CALCIUM 107mg

Roast Beef Heroes

prep: 10 minutes • **cook:** 5 minutes   *POINTS* value: 8

Piled high with roast beef and colorful vegetables, this sandwich is a meal in itself. A generous amount of basil stirred into the mayonnaise gives it a fresh edge, while arugula gives it a peppery bite.

1   (16-ounce) package twin French bread loaves (such as Pepperidge Farm Hot & Crusty)
½   cup light mayonnaise
¼   cup thinly sliced fresh basil
½   teaspoon freshly ground black pepper
¾   pound thinly sliced low-sodium deli roast beef (such as Boar's Head)
1   large tomato, thinly sliced
1   cup thinly sliced red onion
1   large yellow bell pepper, thinly sliced into rings
1   cup arugula leaves

1. Preheat oven, and heat bread according to package directions. Cut each loaf in half horizontally.
2. Combine mayonnaise, basil, and black pepper in a small bowl.
3. Spread mayonnaise mixture over cut sides of bread; layer bottom half of each loaf evenly with roast beef, tomato, onion, bell pepper, and arugula. Replace top halves of bread. Cut each loaf crosswise into 3 sandwiches. **Yield:** 6 servings (serving size: 1 hero).

Per serving: CALORIES 377 (27% from fat); FAT 11.5g (saturated fat 2.1g); PROTEIN 23.4g; CARBOHYDRATES 46.6g; FIBER 3.1g; CHOLESTEROL 37mg; IRON 4.5mg; SODIUM 600mg; CALCIUM 99mg

Menu
POINTS value
per serving: 8

Roast Beef Heroes

Game Plan

1. While oven preheats:
  • Slice basil, tomato, red onion, and bell pepper.

2. While bread heats:
  • Prepare mayonnaise mixture.

3. Assemble sandwiches.

Swiss Cheeseburgers

prep: 4 minutes • **cook:** 11 minutes   *POINTS* value: 7

There's nothing like a good, old-fashioned burger hot off the grill. The melted Swiss cheese and smoky grilled onions make these burgers especially mouthwatering. We only call for lettuce and tomato here, but you can add your favorite burger condiments.

1	pound 93% lean ground beef
1	teaspoon dried Italian seasoning
½	teaspoon salt
1	medium-size sweet onion, cut into 4 (½-inch-thick) slices
	Cooking spray
4	(.8-ounce) slices reduced-fat Swiss cheese
4	(1.5-ounce) white-wheat hamburger buns (such as Nature's Own)
4	green leaf lettuce leaves
4	slices tomato

1. Prepare grill.

2. Combine first 3 ingredients in a medium bowl. Divide mixture into 4 equal portions, shaping each into a ½-inch-thick patty.

3. Place patties and onion slices on a grill rack coated with cooking spray. Grill onion 5 minutes on each side or until tender and lightly browned. Grill patties 5 minutes on each side or until done. Top each patty with 1 slice cheese, and grill 1 minute or until cheese melts.

4. Place 1 patty and 1 onion slice on bottom half of each bun; top with 1 lettuce leaf, 1 tomato slice, and top half of bun. **Yield:** 4 servings (serving size: 1 burger).

Per serving: CALORIES 328 (29% from fat); FAT 10.4g (saturated fat 4.5g); PROTEIN 34.6g; CARBOHYDRATES 28.7g; FIBER 6.2g; CHOLESTEROL 60mg; IRON 4.9mg; SODIUM 706g; CALCIUM 480mg

Flank Steak Wraps

prep: 3 minutes • **cook:** 12 minutes • **other:** 5 minutes   *POINTS* value: 8

Basting the steak during cooking with the sweet and savory mixture of soy sauce, brown sugar, and mirin adds incredible flavor to these wraps.

- 2 tablespoons low-sodium soy sauce
- 2 tablespoons mirin (sweet rice wine)
- 2 tablespoons firmly packed brown sugar
- ½ teaspoon minced garlic
- 1 pound flank steak, trimmed
- Cooking spray
- ¼ cup light mayonnaise
- 1½ teaspoons whole-grain Dijon mustard
- 2 teaspoons lemon juice
- 4 (1.9-ounce) multigrain sandwich wraps (such as Flatout)
- 2 cups torn romaine lettuce
- ½ cup thinly sliced red onion
- 1 red bell pepper, sliced into rings

1. Prepare grill.

2. Combine first 4 ingredients in a small bowl, stirring with a whisk. Set aside.

3. Place steak on grill rack coated with cooking spray. Grill 6 to 8 minutes on each side or until desired degree of doneness, basting frequently with reserved soy sauce mixture. Let steak stand 5 minutes; cut diagonally across grain into thin slices.

4. While steak stands, combine mayonnaise, mustard, and lemon juice. Spread mayonnaise mixture evenly on 1 side of each sandwich wrap. Arrange lettuce, onion, bell pepper, and steak evenly down center of each wrap. Starting at short end, roll up each wrap; cut in half. **Yield:** 4 servings (serving size: 2 wrap halves).

Per serving: CALORIES 381 (33% from fat); FAT 14g (saturated fat 3.1g); PROTEIN 34.9g; CARBOHYDRATES 32.9g; FIBER 9.6g; CHOLESTEROL 43mg; IRON 4mg; SODIUM 874mg; CALCIUM 73mg

Menu
POINTS value
per serving: 8

Flank Steak Wraps

Game Plan
1. While grill heats:
- Slice onion and red bell pepper.
- Prepare soy sauce mixture.

2. Cook steak.

3. While flank steak stands:
- Prepare mayonnaise mixture.

4. Assemble wraps.

Game Plan

1. While broiler preheats:
- Slice bell peppers, onion, squash, and rolls.
- Cook steak.

2. While vegetable mixture cooks:
- Steam squash.
- Toast rolls.

3. Slice steak, and assemble sandwiches.

4. Broil sandwiches.

Open-Faced Steak Sandwiches with Peppers, Onion, and Provolone

prep: 6 minutes • **cook:** 14 minutes   *POINTS* value: 8

You'll need a fork and knife to eat this filling sandwich. Leave the broiler on after toasting the rolls so it will be hot for the final step of melting the cheese.

    Cooking spray
  1 (8-ounce) sirloin steak, 1 inch thick
  ⅜ teaspoon salt, divided
  ⅜ teaspoon freshly ground black pepper, divided
  1 cup sliced red bell pepper
  1 cup sliced yellow bell pepper
  1 cup vertically sliced onion (about 1 small)
  ½ teaspoon dried Italian seasoning
  2 tablespoons balsamic vinegar
  2 (7.5-ounce) ciabatta sandwich rolls, cut in half horizontally
  4 (0.8-ounce) slices reduced-fat provolone cheese

1. Preheat broiler.
2. Heat a large nonstick skillet over medium-high heat. Coat pan with cooking spray. Sprinkle steak with ⅛ teaspoon salt and ⅛ teaspoon black pepper. Add steak to pan, and cook 3 to 4 minutes on each side, or to desired degree of doneness. Remove steak from pan; set aside.
3. Add bell peppers, onion, Italian seasoning, remaining ¼ teaspoon salt, and remaining ¼ teaspoon black pepper to pan; coat vegetable mixture with cooking spray. Cook over medium-high heat, stirring constantly, 4 to 5 minutes or until vegetables are crisp-tender. Stir in vinegar, and remove from heat.
4. While vegetables cook, place roll halves, cut sides up, on a large baking sheet. Broil 2 minutes or until lightly toasted.
5. Cut steaks into thin slices, and arrange evenly on roll halves. Top evenly with vegetable mixture and cheese. Broil 1 minute or until cheese melts. Serve immediately. **Yield:** 4 servings (serving size: 1 sandwich).

Per serving: CALORIES 407 (19% from fat); FAT 8.4g (saturated fat 3.3g); PROTEIN 26.7g; CARBOHYDRATES 54.1g; FIBER 2.6g; CHOLESTEROL 33mg; IRON 4.4mg; SODIUM 768mg; CALCIUM 199mg

Barbecue Chicken Sandwiches

prep: 5 minutes • **cook:** 14 minutes   *POINTS* value: 7

Bread-and-butter pickles are a tasty balance to the smoky barbecue sauce in this updated Southern-style sandwich. Substitute whole leaf lettuce for the shredded lettuce, if you prefer.

  4 (6-ounce) skinless, boneless chicken breast halves
  2 tablespoons salt-free barbecue seasoning (such as Mrs. Dash Grilling Blends for Chicken)
    Cooking spray
  ½ cup (2 ounces) reduced-fat shredded Cheddar cheese
  ½ cup shredded iceberg lettuce
  4 (⅛-inch-thick) slices sweet onion
  4 (1.5-ounce) white-wheat hamburger buns (such as Nature's Own), toasted
  ¼ cup barbecue sauce
 12 bread-and-butter pickle chips

1. Place each chicken breast half between 2 sheets of heavy-duty plastic wrap; pound to ½-inch thickness using a meat mallet or a small heavy skillet. Sprinkle chicken with barbecue seasoning.
2. Heat a large nonstick skillet over medium-high heat. Coat pan with cooking spray. Add chicken to pan; cook 6 minutes on each side or until done. Top chicken with cheese. Cover pan; cook 1 minute or until cheese melts.
3. Arrange ¼ of lettuce and 1 onion slice on bottom half of each bun. Top with 1 chicken breast half, 1 tablespoon barbecue sauce, 3 pickle chips, and top half of bun. **Yield:** 4 servings (serving size: 1 sandwich).

Per serving: CALORIES 375 (18% from fat); FAT 7.3g (saturated fat 3.1g); PROTEIN 48.2g; CARBOHYDRATES 32.2g; FIBER 5.6g; CHOLESTEROL 109mg; IRON 4.1mg; SODIUM 691mg; CALCIUM 392mg

Apple Slaw

prep: 6 minutes   *POINTS* value: 1

Combine ⅓ cup fat-free mayonnaise, 1 tablespoon cider vinegar, and 2 tablespoons sugar in a medium bowl, stirring with a whisk. Add 4 cups packaged coleslaw and 1 golden delicious apple, cored and diced; toss well. **Yield:** 4 servings (serving size: 1¼ cups).

Per serving: CALORIES 78 (7% from fat); FAT 0.6g (saturated fat 0.1g); PROTEIN 0.7g; CARBOHYDRATES 18.8g; FIBER 2.5g; CHOLESTEROL 2mg; IRON 0.3mg; SODIUM 169mg; CALCIUM 23mg

---

Menu
POINTS value
per serving: 8

Barbecue Chicken Sandwiches

Apple Slaw

Game Plan

1. Pound and season chicken.

2. While chicken cooks:
 • Slice onion, and shred lettuce.
 • Toast buns
 • Prepare slaw.

3. Assemble sandwiches.

Menu
POINTS value
per serving: 8

Caesar Chicken Sandwiches

2 peach halves, grilled
POINTS value: 1

Game Plan

1. While chicken marinates:
- Heat grill.
- Halve peaches; slice onion and tomato.
- Shave Parmesan.

2. Grill chicken, onion, buns, and peaches.

3. Assemble sandwiches.

Caesar Chicken Sandwiches

prep: 2 minutes • **cook:** 6 minutes • **other:** 10 minutes   *POINTS* value: 7

To grill peach halves for a sweet side dish or dessert, coat them with cooking spray, and place them on a grill rack coated with cooking spray, cut sides down. Grill for 3 minutes on each side or until the peaches are soft.

  4 (3-ounce) chicken cutlets
  6 tablespoons light Caesar dressing, divided (such as Ken's)
  2 (½-inch-thick) slices red onion
Cooking spray
  4 (1.5-ounce) white-wheat hamburger buns, grilled (such as Nature's Own)
  ½ cup (2 ounces) shaved fresh Parmesan cheese
  4 romaine lettuce leaves
  4 (¼-inch-thick) slices tomato

1. Prepare grill.
2. Combine chicken and ¼ cup dressing in a large zip-top plastic bag. Seal and marinate 10 minutes at room temperature.
3. Remove chicken from bag, discarding marinade. Place chicken and onion on grill rack coated with cooking spray. Cover and grill 3 minutes on each side or until chicken is done and onion is tender. While chicken and onion cook, place buns, cut sides down, on grill rack; toast 1 minute.
4. Brush remaining 2 tablespoons dressing over chicken. Place 1 chicken cutlet on bottom half of each bun; top each cutlet with 2 tablespoons cheese, 1 lettuce leaf, and 1 slice tomato. Separate onion rings; top each sandwich evenly with onion. Replace top halves of buns. **Yield:** 4 servings (serving size: 1 sandwich).

Per serving: CALORIES 332 (30% from fat); FAT 11.9g (saturated fat 3.8g); PROTEIN 31.4g; CARBOHYDRATES 30.5g; FIBER 7.1g; CHOLESTEROL 62mg; IRON 3.8mg; SODIUM 959mg; CALCIUM 429mg

Chicken and Smoked Almond Lettuce Wraps

prep: 10 minutes • **cook:** 7 minutes   *POINTS* value: 5

The sour cream helps cool the heat from the Southwest chipotle seasoning. Salt is often the main ingredient in most seasoning blends. We choose to test with salt-free blends so that we can control the amount of sodium in each dish.

½   cup reduced-fat sour cream
¼   cup chopped green onions (about 2 onions)
2   teaspoons salt-free Southwest chipotle seasoning (such as Mrs. Dash)
¼   teaspoon grated lime rind
1   teaspoon fresh lime juice
Cooking spray
¾   pound skinless, boneless chicken thighs, cut into bite-sized pieces
1   teaspoon salt-free Southwest chipotle seasoning (such as Mrs. Dash)
¼   cup (1-ounce) coarsely chopped smoked almonds
¼   teaspoon salt
8   Bibb lettuce leaves
Chopped fresh cilantro (optional)

1. Combine the first 5 ingredients in a small bowl; stir to combine. Set aside.
2. Heat a large nonstick skillet over medium-high heat. Coat pan with cooking spray. Add chicken and Southwest chipotle seasoning to pan, tossing gently to coat; cook 6 minutes or until done. Remove from heat and stir in almonds and salt. Spoon ½ cup chicken mixture into each lettuce leaf, and top with 2 tablespoons sour cream mixture. Sprinkle with cilantro, if desired. **Yield:** 4 servings (serving size: 2 lettuce wraps).

Per serving: CALORIES 235 (59% from fat); FAT 15.5g (saturated fat 4.5g); PROTEIN 19g; CARBOHYDRATES 4.7g; FIBER 1.2g; CHOLESTEROL 71mg; IRON 1.1mg; SODIUM 274mg; CALCIUM 68mg

Menu
POINTS value
per serving: 7

Chicken and Smoked Almond Lettuce Wraps

½ cup precooked rice with chopped green onions
POINTS value: 2

Game Plan

1. Chop green onions, and prepare sour cream mixture.

2. Cut chicken into bite-sized pieces.

3. While chicken mixture cooks:
• Chop cilantro and almonds.
• Microwave rice according to package directions.

4. Assemble wraps, and toss rice.

pictured on page 119

Asian-Style Turkey Burgers

prep: 7 minutes • **cook:** 10 minutes   *POINTS* value: 5

A burst of ginger, garlic, and soy sauce perks up ground turkey. The secret to moist, tender turkey burgers is tossing the ingredients lightly with your fingers or a fork just until blended.

1   pound 93% lean ground turkey
2   tablespoons finely chopped onion
2   tablespoons finely chopped green bell pepper
1   tablespoon low-sodium soy sauce
2   teaspoons grated fresh ginger
2   garlic cloves, minced
½   teaspoon salt
¼   teaspoon freshly ground black pepper
Cooking spray
4   (1.5-ounce) white-wheat hamburger buns (such as Nature's Own)
Lettuce, tomato, onion (optional)

1. Prepare grill.
2. Combine turkey and next 7 ingredients in a large bowl. Divide mixture into 4 equal portions, shaping each into a ½-inch thick patty.
3. Place patties on a grill rack coated with cooking spray. Grill 5 to 7 minutes on each side or until done. Top bottom half of each bun with lettuce, tomato, and onion, if desired. Top each with 1 patty and top half of bun. **Yield:** 4 servings (serving size: 1 burger).

Per serving: CALORIES 261 (31% from fat); FAT 9.1g (saturated fat 2.5g); PROTEIN 27.5g; CARBOHYDRATES 23.2g; FIBER 5.4g; CHOLESTEROL 65mg; IRON 4.7mg; SODIUM 739mg; CALCIUM 261mg

Avocado-Orange Salad

prep: 6 minutes   *POINTS* value: 2

Combine 3 tablespoons white wine vinegar, 4 teaspoons honey, 1½ teaspoons olive oil, ⅛ teaspoon salt, and ¼ teaspoon freshly ground black pepper in a small bowl; stir well with a whisk. Set aside. Combine 4 cups chopped iceberg lettuce; 2 navel oranges, peeled and sliced; ½ cup sliced avocado; and ¼ cup thinly sliced red onion in a large bowl; drizzle dressing over top and toss gently to coat. **Yield:** 4 servings (serving size: 1⅔ cup).

Per serving: CALORIES 113 (37% from fat); FAT 4.7g (saturated fat 0.7g); PROTEIN 1.5g; CARBOHYDRATES 20.1g; FIBER 5.2g; CHOLESTEROL 0mg; IRON 0.7mg; SODIUM 226mg; CALCIUM 45mg

---

Menu
POINTS value
per serving: 7

Asian-Style Turkey Burgers

Avocado-Orange Salad
POINTS value: 2

Game Plan

1. While grill heats:
• Chop onion and bell pepper.
• Grate ginger, and mince garlic.
• Prepare patties.

2. While patties cook:
• Prepare salad.

3. Assemble burgers.

Soups

Menu
POINTS value
per serving: 6

Provençal Fish Stew

Spicy Roasted Pepper
and Olive Crostini

Game Plan

1. While oven preheats:
 • Slice bread.
 • Chop leek, fennel, and
   parsley; mince garlic.

2. While bread toasts:
 • Cook leek mixture.
 • Chop peppers, olives, and
   basil.
 • Cut fish into pieces.

3. While soup cooks:
 • Assemble crostini.

Provençal Fish Stew

prep: 5 minutes • **cook:** 11 minutes   ***POINTS*** value: 2

**Grouper is a mild fish that absorbs the flavor of the seasonings in
which it cooks, so don't worry about this light stew tasting too fishy.
Don't add the shrimp and fish until the last 3 minutes; they don't
need to cook for long.**

1	teaspoon olive oil
1¼	cups chopped leek
½	cup chopped fennel bulb
1	garlic clove, minced
1	(14.5-ounce) can diced tomatoes
1¼	cups organic vegetable broth
¼	cup dry white wine
3	tablespoons chopped fresh parsley, divided
6	ounces grouper or other firm white fish, cut into 1½-inch pieces
¼	pound peeled and deveined medium shrimp

1. Heat oil in a large Dutch oven over medium-high heat. Add leek, fennel, and
garlic to pan; sauté 4 minutes or until tender. Stir in tomatoes, broth, wine and
1 tablespoon parsley; bring to a boil. Add fish and shrimp; cook 3 minutes or
until done. Sprinkle with remaining 2 tablespoons parsley. **Yield:** 4 servings
(serving size: 1¼ cups).

Per serving: CALORIES 127 (14% from fat); FAT 2g; (saturated fat 0.3g); PROTEIN 14.2g; CARBOHYDRATES 10.5g; FIBER 2.5g; CHOLESTEROL 58mg;
IRON 2.1mg; SODIUM 391mg; CALCIUM 60mg

Spicy Roasted Pepper and Olive Crostini

prep: 3 minutes • **cook:** 8 minutes   ***POINTS*** value: 4

Preheat oven to 350°. Cut 4 ounces of a French bread baguette into 12 diagonally
cut slices; arrange in one layer on a baking sheet. Bake at 350° for 4 minutes; turn
and bake 4 minutes or until golden brown. While bread toasts, combine ½ cup
chopped bottled roasted red peppers, ¼ cup finely chopped jalapeño-stuffed green
olives (about 4), 2 tablespoons chopped fresh basil, 1 medium minced garlic clove,
and 2 teaspoons extra-virgin olive oil in a small bowl. Spoon mixture evenly onto
each bread slice; sprinkle evenly with 1 ounce crumbled feta cheese (about 3 tablespoons). **Yield:** 4 servings (serving size: 3 crostini).

Per serving: CALORIES 168 (38% from fat); FAT 7g; (saturated fat 1.5g); PROTEIN 4.1g; CARBOHYDRATES 22.7g; FIBER 1.9g; CHOLESTEROL 2mg;
IRON 0.6mg; SODIUM 398mg; CALCIUM 27mg

Corn, Potato, and Shrimp Chowder

prep: 3 minutes • **cook:** 14 minutes

POINTS value: 4

Refrigerated mashed potatoes are the secret ingredient to this quick, lightened version of chowder. They add creaminess and thickness to the soup, which eliminates the need for heavy cream. If you prefer a thicker consistency, simply stir the accompanying oyster crackers into each serving.

1 (10-ounce) package frozen whole-kernel corn, thawed and divided
1 cup fat-free milk
2 teaspoons olive oil
¾ cup prechopped onion
¾ cup prechopped tricolor bell pepper mix
1 cup refrigerated mashed potatoes (such as Simply Potatoes)
1 (14-ounce) can fat-free, less-sodium chicken broth
½ pound frozen cooked salad shrimp, thawed
¼ teaspoon salt
½ teaspoon freshly ground black pepper
¼ cup chopped fresh cilantro

1. Place 1 cup corn and milk in a blender; process until almost smooth. Set aside.
2. Heat oil in a Dutch oven over medium-high heat. Add onion and pepper mix to pan; sauté 3 minutes or until tender. Stir in pureed corn mixture, remaining corn, potatoes, and broth. Bring to a boil, stirring frequently. Reduce heat; simmer uncovered, 5 minutes. Add shrimp, salt, and pepper; cook 1 minute or until thoroughly heated. Stir in cilantro. **Yield:** 4 servings (serving size: 1½ cups).

Per serving: CALORIES 225 (16% from fat); FAT 4.1g; (saturated fat 0.6g); PROTEIN 19.1g; CARBOHYDRATES 30.3g; FIBER 3.5g; CHOLESTEROL 112mg; IRON 2.4mg; SODIUM 734mg; CALCIUM 119mg

Menu
POINTS value
per serving: 6

Corn, Potato, and Shrimp Chowder

½ **cup oyster crackers**
POINTS value: 2

Game Plan

1. Puree corn and milk.

2. While onion mixture cooks:
• Chop cilantro.

3. Cook chowder.

Menu
POINTS value
per serving: 7

Quick Bean Soup

1 (2-inch) square cornbread
POINTS value: 3

Game Plan

1. Rinse and drain beans.

2. While onion mixture cooks:
 • Chop tomatoes in can.
 • Measure salsa and cumin.

3. While soup cooks:
 • Chop parsley.

Quick Bean Soup

prep: 7 minutes • **cook:** 13 minutes   *POINTS* value: 4

Save both prep and cleanup time by using kitchen shears to chop the tomatoes right in the can. You can vary the heat with your choice of hot, medium, or mild refrigerated fresh salsa. Serve with store-bought prepared cornbread.

2	teaspoons canola oil
2	cups prechopped onion
¾	cup prechopped green bell pepper
1	cup refrigerated fresh salsa
1	teaspoon ground cumin
1	(16-ounce) can kidney beans, rinsed and drained
1	(16-ounce) can pinto beans, rinsed and drained
1	(15-ounce) can black beans, rinsed and drained
2	(14.5-ounce) cans stewed tomatoes, undrained and chopped
1	(14-ounce) can fat-free, less-sodium chicken broth

Chopped fresh flat-leaf parsley (optional)

1. Heat oil in a Dutch oven over medium-high heat. Add onion and bell pepper to pan; sauté 4 minutes or until tender. Add salsa and remaining ingredients; bring to a boil, stirring occasionally. Cover, reduce heat, and simmer 7 minutes. Garnish with parsley, if desired. **Yield:** 6 servings (serving size: about 1¾ cups).

Per serving: CALORIES 213 (11% from fat); FAT 2.6g; (saturated fat 0.3g); PROTEIN 10.1g; CARBOHYDRATES 36.5g; FIBER 10.3g; CHOLESTEROL 0mg; IRON 3.8mg; SODIUM 859mg; CALCIUM 112mg

pictured on page 123

Chili Picante

prep: 2 minutes • **cook:** 14 minutes   ***POINTS*** value: 4

This dish has the flavor and aroma of a chili that has simmered all day—you're the only one who has to know it hasn't. For a crunchy addition, serve this spicy soup and salad with 1 ounce of baked tortilla chips (12 to 14 chips) for a meal with a total *POINTS* value of 9.

- ¾ pound 93% lean ground beef
- 1 cup prechopped tricolor bell pepper mix
- 1 cup medium picante sauce
- 1 cup water
- 1 (15-ounce) can black beans, rinsed and drained
- 2 teaspoons ground cumin
- ½ cup reduced-fat sour cream

1. Heat a large Dutch oven over medium-high heat. Add beef and peppers to pan; cook until beef is browned, stirring to crumble beef.
2. Add picante sauce and next 3 ingredients to pan; bring to a boil. Reduce heat, and simmer, uncovered, 8 minutes. Ladle into 4 bowls; top evenly with sour cream. **Yield:** 4 servings (serving size: about 1 cup chili and 2 tablespoons sour cream).

Per serving: CALORIES 222 (23% from fat); FAT 5.6g; (saturated fat 2.7g); PROTEIN 23.5g; CARBOHYDRATES 21.7g; FIBER 5g; CHOLESTEROL 55mg; IRON 2.9mg; SODIUM 498mg; CALCIUM 34mg

Menu
POINTS value per serving: 6

Chili Picante

Tex-Mex Layered Salad

Game Plan
1. While ground beef mixture cooks:
- Rinse and drain beans.
- Measure picante sauce, water, and cumin.

2. While chili cooks:
- Prepare salad.

Tex-Mex Layered Salad

prep: 6 minutes   ***POINTS*** value: 2

Combine ⅓ cup reduced-fat sour cream, 2 tablespoons light mayonnaise, and ¼ cup bottled chipotle salsa in a small bowl. Place 1 (8-ounce) bag shredded iceberg lettuce in a large bowl; spoon sour cream mixture over lettuce. Layer 1 cup prediced fresh tomato, ¼ cup finely chopped red onion, and ¼ cup (1 ounce) shredded reduced-fat sharp Cheddar cheese over sour cream mixture. Cover and chill until ready to serve. **Yield:** 4 servings (serving size: 1½ cups).

Per serving: CALORIES 81 (44% from fat); FAT 4g; (saturated fat 2g); PROTEIN 3.4g; CARBOHYDRATES 9.3g; FIBER 1.8g; CHOLESTEROL 12mg; IRON 0.4mg; SODIUM 268mg; CALCIUM 67mg

Menu

POINTS value
per serving: 7

Cincinnati-Style Chili

Game Plan

1. While water for pasta comes to
a boil:
• Cook beef mixture.
• Measure cocoa, brown sugar,
and cinnamon.

2. While pasta cooks:
• Cook chili.
• Chop green onions.

Cincinnati-Style Chili

prep: 2 minutes • **cook:** 18 minutes   *POINTS* value: 7

Cincinnati's famous chili is prepared with an unusual blend of cinnamon and chocolate or cocoa. The people of Cincinnati enjoy their chili spooned over pasta and topped with a combination of chopped onions, shredded Cheddar cheese, and kidney beans. In our version, we've cooked the chili with beans rather than topping it with them.

  11   ounces uncooked whole wheat spaghetti
Cooking spray
   1   pound 93% lean ground beef
  ¾   cup prechopped green bell pepper
  ½   cup prechopped onion
   1   (1.25-ounce) package low-sodium chili seasoning mix (such as McCormick)
1½   teaspoons unsweetened cocoa
   1   teaspoon brown sugar
  ½   teaspoon ground cinnamon
  ½   cup water
   1   (14.5-ounce) can diced tomatoes with garlic and onion
   1   (15-ounce) can dark red kidney beans, rinsed and drained
   6   tablespoons reduced-fat shredded Cheddar cheese
Chopped green onions (optional)

1. Cook pasta according to package directions, omitting salt and fat; drain.
2. While pasta cooks, heat a large nonstick skillet over medium-high heat. Coat pan with cooking spray. Add beef, pepper, and onion to pan; sauté 6 minutes or until browned, stirring to crumble beef. Stir in chili seasoning and next 6 ingredients. Bring to a boil; cover, reduce heat, and simmer 10 minutes, stirring occasionally. Spoon over pasta. Sprinkle each serving with cheese and green onions, if desired.
Yield: 6 servings (serving size: about ¾ cup pasta, about ¾ cup chili, and 1 table-spoon cheese).

Per serving: CALORIES 376 (16% from fat); FAT 6.7g; (saturated fat 2.6g); PROTEIN 28.4g; CARBOHYDRATES 55.2g; FIBER 11.1g; CHOLESTEROL 45mg; IRON 4.5mg; SODIUM 724mg; CALCIUM 100mg

Coconut-Lime Chicken Soup

prep: 3 minutes • **cook:** 13 minutes   *POINTS* value: 4

A cup of light coconut milk added at the end of cooking contributes a velvety texture that's a perfect complement to the sweet, salty, and sour flavors in this Thai dish. Serve with a simple side of sesame-infused stir-fried vegetables to complete this meal.

 2   (14½-ounce) cans fat-free, less-sodium chicken broth
 1   cup presliced mushrooms
 1   small red bell pepper, thinly sliced (about ¾ cup)
 1   tablespoon fish sauce
 1   tablespoon sugar
 ½   teaspoon minced ginger
 2   cups chopped cooked chicken
 1   cup light coconut milk
 ¼   cup fresh basil, thinly sliced
 2   tablespoons fresh lime juice

1. Combine first 6 ingredients in a Dutch oven; bring to a boil. Cover, reduce heat, and simmer 7 minutes. Stir in chicken and coconut milk; simmer 2 minutes or until thoroughly heated. Remove from heat, and stir in basil and lime juice. **Yield:** 4 servings (serving size: 1½ cups).

Per serving: CALORIES 203 (27% from fat); FAT 6g; (saturated fat 3.6g); PROTEIN 29.2g; CARBOHYDRATES 9.2g; FIBER 0.8g; CHOLESTEROL 66mg; IRON 1.4mg; SODIUM 955mg; CALCIUM 19mg

Snow Pea and Carrot Stir-Fry

prep: 1 minute • **cook:** 10 minutes   *POINTS* value: 1

Heat 1 teaspoon dark sesame oil in a large nonstick skillet over medium-high heat. Add 1 (8-ounce) package snow peas and 2 cups matchstick-cut carrot to pan. Cook, stirring often, 8 minutes or until vegetables are crisp-tender. Stir in 1 tablespoon low-sodium soy sauce and remove from heat. **Yield:** 4 servings (serving size: about 1 cup).

Per serving: CALORIES 52 (21% from fat); FAT 1.2g; (saturated fat 0.2g); PROTEIN 1.9g; CARBOHYDRATES 8g; FIBER 2.1g; CHOLESTEROL 0mg; IRON 0.9mg; SODIUM 140mg; CALCIUM 48mg

Menu
POINTS value
per serving: 5

Coconut-Lime Chicken Soup

Snow Pea and Carrot Stir-Fry

Game Plan

1. Slice bell pepper, and mince ginger.

2. While broth mixture comes to a boil and simmers:
 • Prepare stir-fry.
 • Slice basil.
 • Juice lime.

3. Finish cooking soup.

pictured on page 122

Quick Italian Chicken Soup

prep: 3 minutes • **cook:** 17 minutes

POINTS value: 6

This easy soup brims with fresh vegetables, and chopped chicken and beans make it hearty and filling. Serve with the garlicky, crusty Italian bread to soak up the zesty broth.

Menu
POINTS value
per serving: 8

Quick Italian Chicken Soup

Italian Bread with
Garlic-Herb Spread

Game Plan

1. While broiler preheats:
- Cook onion, celery, and garlic.
- Rinse and drain beans.

2. While soup cooks:
- Chop basil.
- Toast bread, and prepare spread.

2	teaspoons olive oil
1	cup prechopped onion
¾	cup prechopped celery
2	garlic cloves, minced
3	cups fat-free, less-sodium chicken broth
1	(14½-ounce) can diced tomatoes with basil, garlic, and oregano
3	tablespoons tomato paste
⅛	teaspoon crushed red pepper
2	cups chopped cooked chicken
1	(15.5-ounce) can no-salt-added Great Northern beans, rinsed and drained
¼	cup chopped fresh basil

1. Heat oil in a Dutch oven over medium-high heat. Add onion, celery, and garlic to pan; sauté 3 minutes or until vegetables are crisp-tender. Add broth, tomatoes, tomato paste, and crushed red pepper; cover, and bring to a boil. Add chicken and beans; reduce heat, and simmer, uncovered, 9 minutes. Stir in basil just before serving. **Yield:** 4 servings (serving size: 2 cups).

Per serving: CALORIES 312 (17% from fat); FAT 5.8g; (saturated fat 1.1g); PROTEIN 30.2g; CARBOHYDRATES 33.9g; FIBER 9.1g; CHOLESTEROL 60mg; IRON 3mg; SODIUM 929mg; CALCIUM 153mg

Italian Bread with Garlic-Herb Spread

prep: 2 minutes • **cook:** 4 minutes

POINTS value: 2

Preheat broiler. Broil 4 (¾-ounce) slices crusty Chicago-style Italian bread 2 minutes on each side or until toasted. While bread toasts, combine 2 tablespoons softened light butter, 1 pressed small garlic clove, and ½ teaspoon dried Italian seasoning. Spread each toasted bread slice with butter mixture. **Yield:** 4 servings (serving size: 1 slice bread and ½ tablespoon butter mixture).

Per serving: CALORIES 91 (43% from fat); FAT 4.3g; (saturated fat 2.4g); PROTEIN 2.1g; CARBOHYDRATES 10.9g; FIBER 0.6g; CHOLESTEROL 7mg; IRON 0.7mg; SODIUM 154mg; CALCIUM 21mg

pictured on page 121

Chicken and Rice Soup with Greens

prep: 2 minutes • **cook:** 18 minutes   *POINTS* value: 4

This is the quintessential nourishing chicken soup. It's chock-full of antioxidants from the colorful veggies and greens, and its ample serving size will leave you feeling warm and satisfied. Add a piece of warm, torn baguette to round out the meal.

1	tablespoon butter
1	cup chopped onion
1	cup chopped carrot
1	cup chopped celery
6	cups fat-free, reduced-sodium chicken broth
1	teaspoon dried thyme
½	teaspoon garlic powder
¼	teaspoon black pepper
6	cups chopped Swiss chard
2	cups chopped cooked chicken
1	(8.8-ounce) pouch microwaveable precooked brown rice (such as Uncle Ben's Ready Rice)

1. Melt butter in a Dutch oven over low heat; add onion, carrot, and celery to pan. Increase heat to medium, and cook 4 minutes, stirring occasionally. Add chicken broth and next 5 ingredients; cover, and bring to a boil.

2. While soup comes to a boil, gently press rice pouch before opening to break grains apart. Add to soup. Reduce heat to medium, and cook uncovered, 10 minutes or until vegetables are tender. **Yield:** 6 servings (serving size: 1⅔ cups).

Per serving: CALORIES 205 (22% from fat); FAT 4.9g; (saturated fat 1.8g); PROTEIN 20.3g; CARBOHYDRATES 20.2g; FIBER 2.7g; CHOLESTEROL 45mg; IRON 1.8mg; SODIUM 712mg; CALCIUM 50mg

Menu
POINTS value
per serving: 6

Quick Chicken and Rice Soup with Greens

1 (1-ounce) torn baguette piece
POINTS value: 2

Game Plan

1. Chop onion, carrot, and celery.

2. While onion mixture cooks:
 • Chop Swiss chard.

3. While broth mixture comes to a boil:
 • Gently press rice pouch.

4. Finish cooking soup.

Santa Fe Chicken Noodle Soup

prep: 5 minutes • **cook:** 12 minutes   *POINTS* value: 5

This Southwestern-inspired chicken noodle soup gets its spicy flavor from green enchilada sauce and cumin, while fresh slices of avocado add richness. You'll only use half of a package of refrigerated pasta for this recipe. To freeze the leftover pasta for another use, carefully wrap it in plastic wrap and aluminum foil before freezing.

½ (9-ounce) package refrigerated linguini pasta
1 (32-ounce) container fat-free, less-sodium chicken broth
2 cups shredded rotisserie chicken breast
1 cup green enchilada sauce (such as Hatch)
1 cup prechopped green bell pepper, onion, and celery mix
⅔ cup fresh or frozen cut corn
1 teaspoon ground cumin
1 peeled avocado, seeded and diced
¼ cup sliced green onions
Lime wedges

1. Remove pasta from package; place on a cutting board. Cut pasta crosswise into 4 sections.
2. Combine chicken broth and next 5 ingredients in a Dutch oven; bring to a boil. Add pasta; cover, reduce heat, and simmer 5 minutes. Ladle soup into 6 bowls; top each evenly with avocado and green onions. Serve with lime wedges. Yield: 6 servings (serving size: about 1¼ cups soup and 1 lime wedge).

Per serving: CALORIES 247 (33% from fat); FAT 9g; (saturated fat 1.7g); PROTEIN 20.9g; CARBOHYDRATES 22.1g; FIBER 3.1g; CHOLESTEROL 52mg; IRON 1.6mg; SODIUM 776mg; CALCIUM 26mg

Desserts

pictured on page 127

Spicy Chocolate Soup

prep: 8 minutes • **cook:** 12 minutes   *POINTS* value: 5

While it may seem like a pricey restaurant dessert, this recipe takes hot chocolate to a different level and can be prepared easily on your stovetop at home. The rich chocolate calms the heat of the ground red pepper, leaving enough spice to delight the palate. Sip this grown-up version of the classic childhood favorite from a mug, or spoon it from a bowl. Serve with 2 savoiardi crispy ladyfinger-like cookies (such as Alessi) for an additional *POINTS* value of 1 per serving.

    2   cups 1% low-fat milk
    ½   vanilla bean, split lengthwise
    ½   (3-inch) cinnamon stick
    3   ounces bittersweet chocolate, chopped
    ¼   cup packed light brown sugar
    ⅛   teaspoon ground red pepper
    ⅛   teaspoon salt
    6   tablespoons fat-free evaporated milk
    1   tablespoon cornstarch
    Frozen fat-free whipped topping, thawed (optional)
    Grated bittersweet chocolate (optional)
    Fresh mint leaves (optional)

1. Combine first 3 ingredients in a large saucepan over medium heat; bring to simmer, stirring frequently.
2. Combine chocolate, brown sugar, pepper, and salt in a medium bowl. Gradually stir about one-fourth of hot milk mixture into chocolate mixture, stirring with a whisk until chocolate melts. Pour chocolate mixture into pan.
3. Combine evaporated milk and cornstarch in a small bowl; stirring with a whisk until smooth. Gradually add cornstarch mixture to chocolate mixture, stirring with a whisk. Continue cooking over medium heat; bring to a boil, and remove from heat. Serve immediately. Top each serving with whipped topping, grated chocolate, and mint leaves, if desired. **Yield:** 4 servings (serving size: ¾ cup).

Per serving: CALORIES 238 (26% from fat); FAT 7g (saturated fat 4.1g); PROTEIN 7.4g; CARBOHYDRATES 39.3g; FIBER 0.2g; CHOLESTEROL 5mg; IRON 0.8mg; SODIUM 185mg; CALCIUM 252mg

Molten Chocolate Lava Cups

prep: 5 minutes • **cook:** 8 minutes, 30 seconds   *POINTS* value: 6

Made with heart-healthy buttery spread instead of real butter and using only minimum amounts of sugar and flour, this ooey-gooey dessert is loaded with dark-chocolate flavor.

     Cooking spray
  ¼ cup sugar, divided
  ½ cup (3 ounces) dark chocolate chips (such as Hershey's Special Dark)
  ¼ cup nonhydrogenated buttery spread (such as Smart Balance)
  ⅓ cup egg substitute
  2 tablespoons all-purpose flour
  1 cup raspberries

1. Preheat oven to 450°.
2. Coat 4 (6-ounce) ramekins or custard cups with cooking spray; sprinkle evenly with 2 tablespoons sugar. Set aside.
3. Combine chocolate and buttery spread in a small microwave-safe bowl. Microwave at HIGH 30 seconds or until melted; stir until smooth.
4. Combine egg substitute and remaining 2 tablespoons sugar in a medium bowl; beat at high speed with a mixer 1 minute or until foamy. Gradually add ¼ cup chocolate mixture, beating until blended. Beat in remaining chocolate mixture and flour. Spoon mixture into prepared ramekins or custard cups.
5. Bake at 450° for 8 minutes or until sides are set, but center is still soft. Invert cakes onto serving plates, and serve with raspberries. **Yield:** 4 servings (serving size: 1 lava cup and ¼ cup raspberries).

Per serving: CALORIES 274 (44% from fat); FAT 14.2g (saturated fat 7.5g); PROTEIN 3.8g; CARBOHYDRATES 37.5g; FIBER 4.1g; CHOLESTEROL 0mg; IRON 2mg; SODIUM 142mg; CALCIUM 15mg

White Chocolate–Strawberry Shortcake

prep: 13 minutes • **cook:** 30 seconds • **other:** 5 minutes   *POINTS* value: 4

Our quick version of strawberry shortcake relies on sponge-cake dessert shells for speed and melted white chocolate and orange rind for heightened flavor. Look for the dessert shells alongside the strawberries in the produce section of your supermarket.

  1   medium navel orange
  2   cups sliced strawberries
  1   tablespoon light brown sugar
 1½   ounces white chocolate, coarsely chopped
 1½   cups fat-free frozen whipped topping, thawed and divided
  1   (6.6-ounce) package sponge-cake dessert shells

1. Grate rind from orange, reserving 1½ teaspoons grated rind; set aside. Slice orange in half, and squeeze ¼ cup juice from 1 orange half; set aside. Reserve remaining orange half for another use. Combine sliced strawberries, 1 teaspoon orange rind, ¼ cup orange juice, and brown sugar; toss gently to coat. Let stand 5 minutes.

2. Place white chocolate in a small microwave-safe bowl. Microwave at HIGH 30 seconds or until chocolate melts; stir. Fold ¼ cup whipped topping into melted chocolate. Fold remaining whipped topping and remaining ½ teaspoon orange rind into chocolate mixture.

3. Place 1 dessert shell onto each of 4 plates. Spoon whipped topping mixture evenly into each dessert shell; top evenly with strawberries. Drizzle with any remaining strawberry juices. **Yield:** 6 servings (serving size: 1 dessert shell, about 3½ tablespoons whipped topping mixture, and about ⅓ cup strawberries).

Per serving: CALORIES 202 (18% from fat); FAT 4g (saturated fat 1.4g); PROTEIN 3g; CARBOHYDRATES 35.5g; FIBER 1.6g; CHOLESTEROL 21mg; IRON 0.7mg; SODIUM 158mg; CALCIUM 33mg

Chai Tea Cream-Filled Angel Food Cake

prep: 17 minutes

POINTS values: 6

This cream-filled angel food cake's highlight is chai tea—a fragrantly spiced, sweetened black tea that includes a combination of cinnamon, cloves, cardamom, and black peppercorns. We've used a sugar-free chai latte tea mix for added sweetness and to keep the calories low.

- ¾ cup (6 ounces) block-style ⅓-less-fat cream cheese, softened
- ¼ cup sugar-free Chai Latte tea mix (such as General Foods International)
- 2 tablespoons light brown sugar
- 1 (8-ounce) container fat-free frozen whipped topping, thawed and divided
- 1 (10-ounce) round sugar-free angel food cake
- 10 (.25-ounce) miniature chocolate-covered toffee candy bars, chopped

1. Combine cream cheese, tea mix, and brown sugar in a large bowl. Beat at medium speed with a mixer 3 minutes until smooth. Gently fold in 1 cup whipped topping. Fold in remaining whipped topping.

2. Remove top ¾ inch of cake using a serrated knife; set aside. Hollow out inside of cake to within ½-inch-thick shell; crumble torn cake.

3. Combine 1 cup cream cheese mixture and crumbled cake in a small bowl; stir in half of chopped candy.

4. Spoon cream cheese-candy mixture into hollowed cake. Replace cake top, pressing down gently. Spread remaining cream cheese mixture over top and sides of cake; sprinkle top and sides with remaining chopped candy. Serve immediately, or cover and chill until ready to serve. **Yield:** 8 servings (serving size: ⅛ of cake).

Per serving: CALORIES 258 (30% from fat); FAT 8.5g (saturated fat 5.4g); PROTEIN 4.5g; CARBOHYDRATES 35.3g; FIBER 0.2g; CHOLESTEROL 17mg; IRON 0.1mg; SODIUM 377mg; CALCIUM 50mg

Banana S'mores

prep: 8 minutes • **cook:** 6 minutes, 45 seconds   *POINTS* value: 4

You don't need a campfire to enjoy this yummy treat! Be sure to watch your marshmallows closely so they don't burn.

    3 tablespoons light brown sugar
 1½ tablespoons unsalted butter
    8 graham cracker squares
    1 teaspoon dark rum (optional)
    1 medium banana, thinly sliced
    3 tablespoons semisweet chocolate mini-chips
  ½ cup miniature marshmallows

1. Preheat oven to 400°. Position 1 oven rack 4 inches from broiler. Position other oven rack in center of oven.
2. Combine brown sugar and butter in a 1-cup glass measure; microwave at HIGH 45 seconds or until butter melts. Stir until sugar dissolves. Place graham cracker squares, sides touching, on a rimmed baking sheet. Drizzle 2 tablespoons of sugar mixture on cracker squares, and spread to edges with back of a spoon. Stir rum into remaining sugar mixture, if desired. Bake squares on oven rack in center of oven at 400° for 5 minutes or until lightly toasted.
3. Preheat broiler.
4. Arrange banana slices on top of squares; drizzle evenly with remaining sugar mixture. Sprinkle evenly with chocolate mini-chips and marshmallows. Broil on oven rack 4 inches from broiler 1 minute or until marshmallows are lightly toasted. **Yield:** 8 servings (serving size: 1 s'more).

Per serving: CALORIES 158 (56% from fat); FAT 9.8g (saturated fat 5.8g); PROTEIN 1g; CARBOHYDRATES 18.2g; FIBER 0.8g; CHOLESTEROL 21mg; IRON 0.5mg; SODIUM 53mg; CALCIUM 8mg

Lemon-Glazed Soft-Baked Cookies

prep: 12 minutes • **cook:** 8 minutes   *POINTS* value: 2

Lemony and luscious, these soft-baked cookies are wonderful with a glass of iced tea in the spring or a cup of hot tea in the winter.

    1   cup low-fat baking mix (such as reduced-fat Bisquick)
    3   tablespoons granulated sugar
    3   tablespoons quick-cooking oats
    3   tablespoons 1% low-fat milk
    2   tablespoons egg substitute
    1   tablespoon butter, melted
    1   teaspoon grated lemon rind
    ½   teaspoon vanilla extract
        Cooking spray
    6   tablespoons powdered sugar
    2   teaspoons fresh lemon juice
    ¼   teaspoon grated lemon rind

1. Preheat oven to 375°.
2. Lightly spoon 1 cup baking mix into a dry measuring cup; level with a knife. Combine baking mix, granulated sugar, and oats in a medium bowl. Add milk and next 4 ingredients, stirring just until dry ingredients are moistened.
3. Drop by level tablespoonfuls 2 inches apart on a baking sheet coated with cooking spray. Bake at 375° for 8 minutes or until cookies are lightly browned around edges.
4. While cookies bake, combine powdered sugar, lemon juice, and lemon rind in a small bowl, stirring with a whisk. Remove cookies to a wire rack, placing wax paper under rack. Drizzle lemon glaze evenly over warm cookies. **Yield:** 12 cookies (serving size: 1 cookie).

Per serving: CALORIES 79 (19% from fat); FAT 1.7g (saturated fat 0.6g); PROTEIN 1.3g; CARBOHYDRATES 14.9g; FIBER 0.3g; CHOLESTEROL 3mg; IRON 0.5mg; SODIUM 123mg; CALCIUM 45mg

Chocolate-Caramel Cheesecake Parfaits

prep: 15 minutes

POINTS value: 8

A sweet cream cheese mixture is layered between a delectable combination of chocolate, caramel, and graham cracker crumbs. Prepare the cream cheese mixture and the cracker crumbs in advance; assemble the parfaits just before serving.

¾ cup (6 ounces) block-style ⅓-less-fat cream cheese, softened
3 tablespoons light brown sugar, divided
2½ tablespoons reduced-fat sour cream
1 tablespoon fat-free milk
1 cup frozen fat-free whipped topping, thawed
½ cup graham cracker crumbs
8 teaspoons fat-free hot fudge topping
8 teaspoons fat-free caramel topping

1. Combine cream cheese, 2 tablespoons brown sugar, sour cream, and milk in a medium bowl; beat with a mixer at medium speed until smooth. Gently fold in whipped topping.

2. Combine remaining 1 tablespoon brown sugar and graham cracker crumbs in a small bowl; stir well. Spoon 2 heaping tablespoons cream cheese mixture into each of 4 (8-ounce) parfait glasses. Top each serving with 1 tablespoon graham cracker crumb mixture and 1 teaspoon each fudge topping and caramel topping. Repeat layers once. Yield: 4 servings (serving size: 1 parfait).

Per serving: CALORIES 294 (32% from fat); FAT 10.3g (saturated fat 6.3g); PROTEIN 6.2g; CARBOHYDRATES 42g; FIBER 0.3g; CHOLESTEROL 31mg; IRON 0.5mg; SODIUM 357mg; CALCIUM 57mg

pictured on page 125

Double-Chocolate Pudding

prep: 5 minutes • **cook:** 11 minutes

POINTS value: 4

In just a fraction more time, you can make this smooth homemade pudding instead of opening a box of instant. The intense chocolate flavor and velvety texture is well worth the few extra minutes.

   2   cups fat-free milk
   1   large egg, lightly beaten
  ½   cup sugar
  ¼   cup unsweetened cocoa
   3   tablespoons cornstarch
  ⅛   teaspoon salt
   2   ounces semisweet chocolate, chopped
   2   teaspoons vanilla extract
   1   teaspoon butter

1. Combine first 6 ingredients in a medium, heavy saucepan, stirring with a whisk. Bring to a boil over medium heat, stirring constantly with a whisk. Reduce heat, and simmer 1 minute or until thick.

2. Remove pan from heat; add chocolate, vanilla, and butter, stirring with a whisk until mixture is smooth. Serve warm, or cover surface of pudding with plastic wrap, and chill until ready to serve. Yield: 6 servings (serving size: ½ cup).

Per serving: CALORIES 185 (27% from fat); FAT 5.6g (saturated fat 3g); PROTEIN 5.5g; CARBOHYDRATES 31.4g; FIBER 1.5g; CHOLESTEROL 33mg; IRON 1.2mg; SODIUM 109mg; CALCIUM 115mg

Cinnamon-Spiked Brown Rice Pudding

prep: 5 minutes • **cook:** 8 minutes

POINTS value: 6

Satisfy your sweet tooth and add a serving of whole grains to your diet with this creamy low-fat rice pudding. The variations for this easy dessert are endless—substitute cooked barley, quinoa, or even bulgur for the rice; or use dried blueberries, raisins, or dried cherries instead of the cranberries.

1 (8.8-ounce) pouch microwaveable cooked whole grain brown rice (such as Uncle Ben's Ready Rice)
1 (12-ounce) can low-fat evaporated milk
⅓ cup packed light brown sugar
¼ cup sweetened dried cranberries
1 teaspoon vanilla extract
½ teaspoon ground cinnamon
⅛ teaspoon salt
⅓ cup egg substitute
2 teaspoons cornstarch
4 cinnamon sticks (optional)

1. Microwave rice according to package directions.
2. While rice cooks, combine evaporated milk and next 5 ingredients in a medium saucepan; bring to a boil, stirring with a whisk. Reduce heat to medium; add rice to pan, and cook 3 minutes, stirring often with a whisk. Reduce heat to low.
3. Combine egg substitute and cornstarch in a small bowl, stirring with a whisk. Add ¼ cup milk mixture to cornstarch mixture, stirring constantly with a whisk. Return milk-cornstarch mixture to pan. Cook over low heat until thick (1 minute), stirring constantly. Remove from heat. Spoon pudding evenly into 4 serving bowls. Garnish each serving with a cinnamon stick, if desired. **Yield:** 4 servings (serving size: ¾ cup).

Per serving: CALORIES 283 (12% from fat); FAT 4g (saturated fat 1.7g); PROTEIN 10.1g; CARBOHYDRATES 52.1g; FIBER 1.5g; CHOLESTEROL 14mg; IRON 1.3mg; SODIUM 213mg; CALCIUM 246mg

Ginger-Pear Tartlets

prep: 4 minutes • **cook:** 14 minutes   *POINTS* value: 1

The sweet, warm fruit filling and the gingersnap crumb topping will remind you of fall.

  1 (1.9-ounce) package miniature phyllo shells
  1 tablespoon butter
  5 gingersnap cookies, finely crushed
  1 large ripe pear, peeled, cored, and chopped
  3 tablespoons chopped dates
  ¾ cup pear nectar
  1 tablespoon honey
  ¾ teaspoon fresh lemon juice
  ¼ teaspoons ground cinnamon

1. Preheat oven to 350°.
2. Arrange phyllo shells on baking sheet; bake at 350° for 5 minutes or until lightly browned.
3. Melt butter in a large nonstick skillet over medium-high heat. Add gingersnap crumbs to pan; cook 1 minute, stirring frequently. Remove crumb mixture from pan, and set aside. Add pear and remaining ingredients to pan. Bring to a boil over medium heat, stirring frequently. Reduce heat, and simmer until pear is tender and most of liquid evaporates. Add half of crumb mixture to pan, stirring until crumbs dissolve. Remove from heat. Spoon pear mixture evenly into phyllo shells. Sprinkle evenly with remaining crumb mixture. Serve warm or at room temperature.
Yield: 15 servings (serving size: 1 tartlet).

Per serving: CALORIES 58 (29% from fat); FAT 1.9g (saturated fat 0.5g); PROTEIN 0.3g; CARBOHYDRATES 10.5g; FIBER 0.7g; CHOLESTEROL 2mg; IRON 0.4mg; SODIUM 33mg; CALCIUM 5mg

Raspberry-Lime Cream Cheese Tartlets

prep: 7 minutes

POINTS value: 1

These bite-sized desserts are ideal finger food for casual entertaining. To make these tartlets ahead, prepare the filling, and chill until you are ready to assemble.

- ½ cup (4 ounces) block-style ⅓-less-fat cream cheese, softened
- ¼ cup powdered sugar
- 1 tablespoon fat-free milk
- 2 teaspoons grated lime rind
- 1 (1.9-ounce) package miniature phyllo shells
- 15 small raspberries (about ¼ cup)

1. Combine first 4 ingredients in a small bowl; beat with a mixer at medium speed 2 minutes or until smooth.

2. Spoon cream cheese mixture evenly into phyllo shells. Top each tartlet with 1 raspberry. Yield: 15 servings (serving size: 1 tartlet).

Per serving: CALORIES 44 (51% from fat); FAT 2.5g (saturated fat 1.1g); PROTEIN 0.9g; CARBOHYDRATES 0.5g; FIBER 0.3g; CHOLESTEROL 5.4mg; IRON 0.2mg; SODIUM 46mg; CALCIUM 9mg

Cinnamon-Pecan Apples

prep: 9 minutes • **cook:** 8 minutes

POINTS value: 3

Don't reserve pumpkin pie spice for pumpkin or sweet potato desserts alone; this blend of cinnamon, ginger, nutmeg, and allspice is just as tasty on apples.

- 4 small Fuji apples, peeled and cored (about 1½ pounds)
- 4 teaspoons nonhydrogenated buttery spread (such as Smart Balance)
- 4 teaspoons light brown sugar
- 1 tablespoon maple syrup
- 1½ teaspoons pumpkin pie spice
- 4 teaspoons chopped pecans, toasted
- ½ cup vanilla low-fat Greek yogurt

1. Arrange apples in a circular pattern in a glass pie plate. Combine buttery spread, brown sugar, maple syrup, and pumpkin pie spice in a small bowl. Spoon buttery spread mixture evenly into each apple. Cover apples with wax paper and microwave at HIGH 8 minutes or until tender. Cut apples into wedges. Sprinkle apple wedges evenly with pecans and top with yogurt. **Yield:** 4 servings (serving size: 1 apple, about 1 tablespoon sauce, 1 teaspoon pecans, and 2 tablespoons yogurt).

Per serving: CALORIES 186 (28% from fat); FAT 5.8g (saturated fat 1.6g); PROTEIN 3.5g; CARBOHYDRATES 33.4g; FIBER 4.4g; CHOLESTEROL 2mg; IRON 0.5mg; SODIUM 45mg; CALCIUM 54mg

Poached Apricots with Crumbled Feta, Honey, and Walnuts

prep: 2 minutes • **cook:** 18 minutes

POINTS value: 6

Be sure to look for cranberry juice labeled "100% juice," which contains no added sugar. Cranberry juice cocktail contains a higher amount of sugar and will boost the *POINTS* value by 1 per serving as well as make this dish too sweet.

1	cup dried apricots
1½	cups cranberry juice
1	tablespoon Grand Marnier or other orange-flavored liqueur
1	tablespoon sugar
⅛	teaspoon salt
¼	cup crumbled reduced-fat feta cheese
¼	cup chopped walnuts, toasted
¼	cup honey

1. Combine first 5 ingredients in a medium saucepan; cover, and bring to a boil. Reduce heat, and simmer 15 minutes or until liquid is syrupy.

2. Spoon ¼ of apricot mixture into each of 4 dessert dishes; sprinkle each serving evenly with cheese and walnuts. Drizzle evenly with honey. **Yield:** 4 servings (serving size: about 8 apricots, 2 tablespoons syrup, 1 tablespoon cheese, 1 tablespoon walnuts, and 1 tablespoon honey).

Per serving: CALORIES 330 (16% from fat); FAT 5.9g (saturated fat 1.2g); PROTEIN 4.1g; CARBOHYDRATES 63g; FIBER 3.1g; CHOLESTEROL 3mg; IRON 2.6mg; SODIUM 203mg; CALCIUM 68mg

pictured on page 126

Broiled Berries and Peaches with Ice Cream

prep: 5 minutes • **cook:** 7 minutes   *POINTS* value: 4

Warm, saucy blueberries, raspberries, and peaches combine to form a deliciously simple dessert. Substitute freshly squeezed orange juice for the Grand Marnier, if you prefer.

   ⅔   cup blueberries
   ⅔   cup raspberries
   4   peaches, halved and pitted
   2   tablespoons Grand Marnier or other orange-flavored liqueur
   ⅛   cup packed light brown sugar
   2   cups vanilla fat-free ice cream (such as Edy's)

1. Preheat broiler.

2. Arrange blueberries, raspberries, and peaches, cut sides up, on a foil-lined jelly-roll pan; drizzle evenly with liqueur, and sprinkle evenly with brown sugar.

3. Broil 7 to 8 minutes or until peaches are lightly browned. Divide broiled fruit into each of 4 dessert bowls; top evenly with ice cream. **Yield:** 4 servings (serving size: 2 peach halves, about 3 tablespoons berries, and ½ cup ice cream).

Per serving: CALORIES 251 (3% from fat); FAT 0.7g (saturated fat 0g); PROTEIN 4.6g; CARBOHYDRATES 56.5g; FIBER 4.3g; CHOLESTEROL 0mg; IRON 0.9mg; SODIUM 50mg; CALCIUM 103mg

Blueberry Fool

prep: 14 minutes • **cook:** 4 minutes

POINTS value: 5

We've updated the traditional English fool—typically made with pureed fruit and whipping cream—by creating a sauce with fresh, vibrant blueberries that tops a fluffy mixture of light cream cheese, light sour cream, and fat-free whipped topping.

1	cup blueberries
2	tablespoons water
1	tablespoon granulated sugar
1	teaspoon fresh lemon juice
¾	cup (6 ounces) block-style ⅓-less-fat cream cheese, softened
3	tablespoons powdered sugar
2½	tablespoons light sour cream
1	tablespoon fat-free milk
1	teaspoon vanilla extract
1	cup frozen fat-free whipped topping, thawed

1. Combine first 4 ingredients in a small saucepan over medium-high heat. Cook 4 minutes or until sauce thickens. Remove from heat. Place pan in a large ice-filled bowl 5 minutes or until berry sauce comes to room temperature, stirring occasionally.

2. Combine cream cheese and next 4 ingredients in a medium bowl. Beat with a mixer at medium speed 3 minutes or until smooth. Gently fold in whipped topping. Gently fold in ⅓ cup berry sauce.

3. Divide cream cheese mixture evenly among 4 dessert dishes; top each evenly with remaining berry sauce. Yield: 4 servings (serving size: ½ cup cream cheese mixture and about 2 teaspoons berry sauce).

Per serving: CALORIES 207 (43% from fat); FAT 9.9g (saturated fat 6.6g); PROTEIN 5.3g; CARBOHYDRATES 23.3g; FIBER 0.9g; CHOLESTEROL 34mg; IRON 0.1mg; SODIUM 212mg; CALCIUM 38mg

Sherry Figs with Mascarpone

prep: 5 minutes • **cook:** 11 minutes

POINTS value: 5

The sherry mixture used to poach the figs is reduced to form a silky sauce that's drizzled over the mascarpone mixture. A blend of mascarpone and Greek fat-free yogurt lends a custardlike texture without the trouble of preparing custard.

½ cup cream sherry
2½ tablespoons honey, divided
1 (3-inch) cinnamon stick
½ cup Greek fat-free yogurt
¼ cup mascarpone cheese
10 fresh figs (about ½ pound)

1. Combine sherry, 1 tablespoon honey, and cinnamon stick in a medium saucepan. Bring to a boil; cook 7 minutes or until slightly thickened. Remove and discard cinnamon stick.

2. While sherry mixture cooks, combine remaining 1½ tablespoons honey, yogurt, and cheese in a small bowl, stirring with a whisk.

3. Add figs to sherry mixture, tossing gently to coat. Cook 1 minute or just until thoroughly heated.

4. Spoon yogurt mixture evenly into 4 long-stemmed dessert glasses or dessert dishes. Top each serving evenly with fig mixture. **Yield:** 4 servings (serving size: 5 fig halves, 3 tablespoons yogurt mixture, and 1½ teaspoons sauce).

Per serving: CALORIES 238 (50% from fat); FAT 13.2g (saturated fat 7.1g); PROTEIN 5g; CARBOHYDRATES 23.3g; FIBER 1.7g; CHOLESTEROL 35mg; IRON 0.4mg; SODIUM 29mg; CALCIUM 82mg

Cookie-Stuffed Nectarines

prep: 5 minutes • **cook:** 10 minutes   *POINTS* value: 4

Light ice cream can be hard to scoop right out of the freezer. Try microwaving it for 20 seconds to soften it just enough for scooping.

1½	teaspoons lemon juice
3	medium nectarines, halved and pitted
¾	cup peach nectar
1	tablespoon light brown sugar
3	(¾-ounce) almond biscotti, crushed (about ⅔ cup crumbs)
2	tablespoons peach fruit spread
⅛	teaspoon ground cinnamon
3	cups light vanilla or caramel ice cream

1. Preheat oven to 475°.

2. Drizzle lemon juice evenly over nectarines. Combine peach nectar and brown sugar in a small bowl, stirring until sugar dissolves. Pour nectar mixture into an 8-inch square baking dish; toss nectarines in nectar mixture. Arrange nectarines, cut sides up, in dish. Bake at 475° for 5 minutes.

3. While nectarines bake, combine biscotti crumbs, peach spread, and cinnamon in a small bowl. Spoon crumb mixture evenly into center of each nectarine half, mounding slightly. Bake 5 additional minutes or until crumb mixture is lightly browned and nectarines are tender. Serve with ice cream and drizzle evenly with sauce in dish. **Yield:** 6 servings (serving size: 1 nectarine half, ½ cup ice cream, and 2 tablespoons plus 2 teaspoons sauce).

Per serving: CALORIES 214 (22% from fat); FAT 5.3g (saturated fat 2.5g); PROTEIN 4.6g; CARBOHYDRATES 40g; FIBER 1.2g; CHOLESTEROL 30mg; IRON 0.3mg; SODIUM 81mg; CALCIUM 64mg

Grilled Peaches with Balsamic Vinegar and Vanilla Ice Cream

prep: 9 minutes • **cook:** 5 minutes   *POINTS* value: 4

If you're planning to heat up your grill to cook dinner, then save time and effort by grilling your dessert, too. A splash of tangy, sweet balsamic vinegar enhances the flavor of juicy, grilled peaches.

    4   large peaches, halved and pitted
    2   tablespoons butter, melted
  Cooking spray
  1½   tablespoons dark brown sugar
    2   cups fat-free vanilla ice cream (such as Edy's)
    4   teaspoons balsamic vinegar

1. Prepare grill.

2. Lightly brush cut sides of peaches with melted butter. Place peach halves, cut sides down, on grill rack coated with cooking spray. Cook 3 minutes or until grill marks are visible, turning peaches using tongs. Spoon about 1 teaspoon brown sugar into center of each peach half. Cover with grill lid, and grill 2 minutes or until sugar melts and peaches are thoroughly heated.

3. Place 2 peach halves in each of 4 dessert bowls; top evenly with ice cream. Drizzle evenly with balsamic vinegar. **Yield:** 4 servings (serving size: 2 peach halves, ½ cup ice cream, and 1 teaspoon balsamic vinegar).

Per serving: CALORIES 226 (24% from fat); FAT 6.1g (saturated fat 3.6g); PROTEIN 4.5g; CARBOHYDRATES 39.9g; FIBER 3.3g; CHOLESTEROL 15mg; IRON 0.5mg; SODIUM 109mg; CALCIUM 117mg

Strawberry-Rhubarb Compote with Ice Cream

prep: 8 minutes • **cook:** 7 minutes • **other:** 5 minutes   *POINTS* value: 3

Sweet strawberries are a classic partner to sour rhubarb. Prepare this winning compote during the spring months when strawberries and rhubarb are at their peaks.

   1   pound strawberries, sliced
   2   cups (½-inch) sliced rhubarb (about ½ pound)
  ⅓   cup packed light brown sugar
   2   tablespoons water
   4   cups light vanilla ice cream (such as Edy's)

1. Combine first 4 ingredients in a medium saucepan; bring to a boil. Reduce heat to medium, and simmer 6 to 7 minutes or until rhubarb softens. Remove from heat, and let stand 5 minutes. Serve warm strawberry mixture over ice cream.
Yield: 8 servings (serving size: about ⅓ cup compote and ½ cup ice cream).

Per serving: CALORIES 167 (18% from fat); FAT 3.4g (saturated fat 2g); PROTEIN 3.8g; CARBOHYDRATES 31.4g; FIBER 1.8g; CHOLESTEROL 18mg; IRON 0.6mg; SODIUM 54mg; CALCIUM 147mg

Minted Fruit Compote

Spoon the fruit mixture into martini glasses or stemmed dessert glasses for a quick, tasty, and elegant ending to a summertime supper.

- ½ cup sparkling water, chilled and divided (such as Pellegrino)
- 3 tablespoons honey
- 3 cups cubed cantaloupe
- 1 cup blueberries
- 2 tablespoons thinly sliced fresh mint

1. Combine ¼ cup sparkling water and honey in a large bowl, stirring until smooth. Add remaining ¼ cup sparking water, cantaloupe, blueberries, and mint; toss gently to coat. **Yield:** 4 servings (serving size: 1 cup).

Per serving: CALORIES 115 (3% from fat); FAT 0.4g (saturated fat 0.1g); PROTEIN 1.5g; CARBOHYDRATES 29.4g; FIBER 1g; CHOLESTEROL 0mg; IRON 0.5mg; SODIUM 24mg; CALCIUM 22mg

Tropical Fruit Compote with Angel Food Cake

prep: 11 minutes

POINTS value: 3

Try serving this refreshing combination of tropical fruit by itself or over light ice cream. In this recipe, rum is used for a little added flavor, but if you prefer to omit it, this dessert will still taste delicious.

- ½ cup mango nectar
- 1 tablespoon sugar
- 1 tablespoon white rum
- 1 teaspoon fresh lime juice
- 1 cup cubed fresh pineapple
- 1 cup cubed kiwifruit (2 large)
- 1 cup cubed mango (1 large)
- 1 (10-ounce) round sugar-free angel food cake

1. Combine first 4 ingredients in a medium bowl; stirring with a whisk until sugar dissolves.

2. Add pineapple, kiwi, and mango; toss gently to coat. Cut cake into 6 slices. Spoon fruit mixture evenly over each slice. **Yield:** 6 servings (serving size: 1 slice cake and ½ cup compote).

Per serving: CALORIES 185 (1% from fat); FAT 0.3g (saturated fat 0g); PROTEIN 3.2g; CARBOHYDRATES 43g; FIBER 1.9g; CHOLESTEROL 0mg; IRON 0.3mg; SODIUM 301mg; CALCIUM 54mg

pictured on page 124

Fresh Pineapple-Lime Dessert Salsa

prep: 8 minutes • **other:** 10 minutes   ***POINTS*** value: 1

Crystallized ginger contributes to the sweet and spicy notes of this pineapple salsa. Look for it in the Asian-food section of your supermarket. Try the salsa spooned over ½ cup blood orange or strawberry sorbet or light vanilla ice cream for an additional *POINTS* value of 2 per serving.

    2   cups chopped fresh pineapple
1½   tablespoons chopped fresh mint
1½   tablespoons honey
    2   teaspoons chopped crystallized ginger
    2   teaspoons grated fresh lime rind
1½   tablespoons fresh lime juice
Blood orange sorbet (optional)
Garnish: fresh mint sprigs (optional)

1. Combine all ingredients in a medium bowl; let stand 10 minutes to develop juices. Spoon each serving over sorbet and garnish with mint, if desired. **Yield:** 8 servings (serving size: ¼ cup salsa).

Per serving: CALORIES 37 (5% from fat); FAT 0.2g (saturated fat 0g); PROTEIN 0.3g; CARBOHYDRATES 9.9g; FIBER 0.5g; CHOLESTEROL 0mg; IRON 0.3mg; SODIUM 1mg; CALCIUM 8mg

Strawberries and Mint with Lemon Simple Syrup

prep: 3 minutes • **cook:** 5 minutes • **other:** 10 minutes   *POINTS* value: 1

Freshly ground black pepper may seem like an odd ingredient in a dessert, but in this recipe, it accentuates the flavor of the sweet, juicy strawberries and offers a deliciously unexpected hint of spice. To make this recipe quick to prepare, halve the strawberries while the lemon syrup stands.

> 1 tablespoon sugar
> 1 tablespoon water
> 1 tablespoon fresh lemon juice
> 1 tablespoon honey
> 3 cups halved strawberries
> 1 tablespoon chopped fresh mint
> ⅛ teaspoon freshly ground black pepper

1. Combine first 4 ingredients in a small saucepan. Bring to a boil; cook 3 minutes or until slightly syrupy. Remove from heat. Let stand 10 minutes.

2. Combine strawberries, mint, and pepper in a large bowl. Add syrup; toss gently to coat. **Yield:** 4 servings (serving size: ¾ cup).

Per serving: CALORIES 69 (5% from fat); FAT 0.4g (saturated fat 0g); PROTEIN 0.9g; CARBOHYDRATES 17.5g; FIBER 2.6g; CHOLESTEROL 0mg; IRON 0.6mg; SODIUM 2mg; CALCIUM 22mg

Affogato

prep: 4 minutes • **cook:** 3 minutes

Affogato is an Italian-style ice cream dessert that's been drowned with espresso and liqueur. Here, we've dressed up this treat with chocolate shavings and made the dousing of Kahlúa optional.

  2 tablespoons instant espresso granules
  ½ cup boiling water
  2 cups light vanilla ice cream (such as Edy's)
  4 teaspoons Kahlúa, optional
  2 tablespoons shaved bittersweet chocolate

1. Combine espresso granules and boiling water, stirring until granules dissolve.

2. Place ½ cup ice cream in each of 4 dessert bowls. Drizzle each serving with 2 tablespoons espresso, 1 teaspoon Kahlúa, if desired, and ½ tablespoon chocolate.

Yield: 4 servings (serving size: 1 affogato).

Per serving: CALORIES 127 (36% from fat); FAT 5.2g (saturated fat 3g); PROTEIN 3.3g; CARBOHYDRATES 18.9g; FIBER 0.3g; CHOLESTEROL 0mg; IRON 0.2mg; SODIUM 50mg; CALCIUM 62mg

pictured on page 128

Strawberry Ice Cream Sundaes

prep: 6 minutes • **cook:** 4 minutes

POINTS value: 4

Store-bought round vanilla ice cream sandwiches make this cool dessert a cinch to prepare. For more chocolate flavor, substitute chocolate ice cream sandwiches for the vanilla.

¼ cup light chocolate syrup, divided
4 (4-ounce) low-fat round vanilla ice cream sandwiches (such as Weight Watchers)
¼ cup strawberry preserves
½ cup canned refrigerated light whipped topping (such as Reddi wip)
4 strawberries (optional)

1. Drizzle ½ tablespoon syrup on each of 4 dessert plates. Arrange 1 ice cream sandwich on each plate. Top each sandwich with 1 tablespoon preserves, 2 tablespoons whipped topping, and ½ tablespoon syrup. Top with a strawberry, if desired. **Yield:** 4 servings (serving size: 1 sundae).

Per serving: CALORIES 230 (12% from fat); FAT 3.1g (saturated fat 1g); PROTEIN 4.1g; CARBOHYDRATES 53g; FIBER 4g; CHOLESTEROL 0mg; IRON 0.1mg; SODIUM 158mg; CALCIUM 82mg

Index

10 Simple Side Dishes

Vegetable	Servings	Preparation	Cooking Instructions
Asparagus	3 to 4 per pound	Snap off tough ends. Remove scales, if desired.	To steam: Cook, covered, on a rack above boiling water 2 to 3 minutes. To boil: Cook, covered, in a small amount of boiling water 2 to 3 minutes or until crisp-tender.
Broccoli	3 to 4 per pound	Remove outer leaves and tough ends of lower stalks. Wash; cut into spears.	To steam: Cook, covered, on a rack above boiling water 5 to 7 minutes or until crisp-tender.
Carrots	4 per pound	Scrape; remove ends, and rinse. Leave tiny carrots whole; slice large carrots.	To steam: Cook, covered, on a rack above boiling water 8 to 10 minutes or until crisp-tender. To boil: Cook, covered, in a small amount of boiling water 8 to 10 minutes or until crisp-tender.
Cauliflower	4 per medium head	Remove outer leaves and stalk. Wash. Break into florets.	To steam: Cook, covered, on a rack above boiling water 5 to 7 minutes or until crisp-tender.
Corn	4 per 4 large ears	Remove husks and silks. Leave corn on the cob, or cut off kernels.	Cook, covered, in boiling water to cover 8 to 10 minutes (on cob) or in a small amount of boiling water 4 to 6 minutes (kernels).
Green beans	4 per pound	Wash; trim ends, and remove strings. Cut into 1½-inch pieces.	To steam: Cook, covered, on a rack above boiling water 5 to 7 minutes. To boil: Cook, covered, in a small amount of boiling water 5 to 7 minutes or until crisp-tender.
Potatoes	3 to 4 per pound	Scrub; peel, if desired. Leave whole, slice, or cut into chunks.	To boil: Cook, covered, in boiling water to cover 30 to 40 minutes (whole) or 15 to 20 minutes (slices or chunks). To bake: Bake at 400° for 1 hour or until done.
Snow peas	4 per pound	Wash; trim ends, and remove tough strings.	To steam: Cook, covered, on a rack above boiling water 2 to 3 minutes. Or sauté in cooking spray or 1 teaspoon oil over medium-high heat 3 to 4 minutes or until crisp-tender.
Squash, summer	3 to 4 per pound	Wash; trim ends, and slice or chop.	To steam: Cook, covered, on a rack above boiling water 6 to 8 minutes. To boil: Cook, covered, in a small amount of boiling water 6 to 8 minutes or until crisp-tender.
Squash, winter *(including acorn, butternut, and buttercup)*	2 per pound	Rinse; cut in half, and remove all seeds. Leave in halves to bake, or peel and cube to boil.	To boil: Cook cubes, covered, in boiling water 20 to 25 minutes. To bake: Place halves, cut sides down, in a shallow baking dish; add ½ inch water. Bake, uncovered, at 375° for 30 minutes. Turn and season, or fill; bake an additional 20 to 30 minutes or until tender.